P9-DIJ-755

THE PARABLES OF JESUS

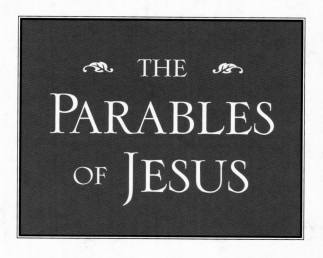

THE PARABLES OF JESUS

And Their Place in Christian Art

ABIGAIL WILLIS

PENGUIN STUDIO

PENGUIN STUDIO
Published by the Penguin Group
Penguin Putnam Inc., 375 Hudson Street, New York, New York 10014, U.S.A.
Penguin Books Ltd, 27 Wrights Lane, London W8 5TZ, England
Penguin Books Australia Ltd, Ringwood, Victoria, Australia
Penguin Books Canada Ltd, 10 Alcorn Avenue, Toronto, Ontario, Canada M4V 3B2
Penguin Books Ltd (N.Z.) 182–190 Wairau Road, Auckland 10, New Zealand

Penguin Books Ltd, Registered Offices: Harmondsworth, Middlesex, England

First published in 1998 by Penguin Studio, a member of Penguin Putnam Inc.

1 3 5 7 9 10 8 6 4 2

Library of Congress Cataloging-in-Publication Data
Willis, Abigail.
The parables of Jesus / Abigail Willis.
p.   cm.
1. Jesus Christ—Parables. 2. Bible. N.T. Gospels—Criticism, interpretation, etc.
3. Christian art and symbolism. I. Bible. N.T. Gospels. English. Authorized.
Selections. 1998. II. Title.
BT375.2.W535 1998   97-34879
226.8—dc21

Printed and bound in Great Britain by Butler & Tanner Ltd., Frome and London
Set in Bembo
Designed by Pei Koay and Helene Berinsky

FRONTISPIECE: CHRIST TEACHING THE PARABLE OF THE GOOD SAMARITAN
(DETAIL FROM WINDOW AT CHARTRES CATHEDRAL)
c. 1210, stained glass
Photo: Copyright Sonia Halliday and Laura Lushington

A rare image of Christ teaching a parable, in which one of his audience is identified—by way of an explanatory caption and his Jewish headdress—as a Pharisee. The significance of this becomes evident in its opposite panel, which shows the priest and Levite passing by the wounded traveler.

For my parents,

John and Belinda

❧ ACKNOWLEDGMENTS ❧

Alexander Ballinger

Kate Chenevix-Tench

The Conway Library, Courtauld
    Institute of Art, London

The Department of Prints and
    Drawings, the British Museum

Dr. Cathy Gordon

Colum Hourihane

Matthew Imms

Sophie Janson

Richard Jefferies, the Watts Gallery,
    Compton, Surrey

Derek Kendall

Gayle Mault, the National Trust Photo
    Library, London

Malcolm Miller

Mr. O'Connor, Lincoln Cathedral

Pitkin Publications

Christopher Sweet

Caroline and Sebastian Thomas

Barbara Thompson, the Witt Library,
    Courtauld Institute of Art, London

Leslie Waddington

June Warrington

Phoebe Whitton, Sonia Halliday
    Photographs

John and Belinda Willis

The Witt Computer Index, Courtauld
    Institute of Art, London

CONTENTS

INTRODUCTION

"And he taught them many things in parables."

Much of Jesus' earthly career was devoted to teaching, and as we learn from the Gospels, it was as a teacher and healer that he first found fame in his native land. Like every good teacher, Jesus had a favorite tactic to help capture his pupils' attention and to convey his points more effectively. The method Jesus used—and made his own—was the parable. Originally transmitted by word of mouth, first by Jesus and then by his disciples, Jesus' teachings were subsequently written down by the so-called Synoptic Gospelists (Matthew, Mark, and Luke), and the parables have thus remained a valuable teaching tool for the Church itself. Although well-known parables such as the Good Samaritan and the Prodigal Son are often simplified into children's stories, the ambiguous meanings and provocative content of many of the parables has continued to challenge readers, just as they engaged Jesus' original audience, two thousand years ago. The powerful narratives they incorporate have sometimes encouraged the parables to be regarded simply as moralizing short stories, as "earthly stories with a heavenly message." This does them a disservice, denying them their full spiritual and artistic significance—centuries of attempts to interpret the parables surely testify to their complexity.

WILLIAM HOLMAN HUNT, *THE LIGHT OF THE WORLD*
1851–53, retouched 1858, 1886, oil on canvas over panel
By permission of the Warden and Fellows of Keble College, Oxford

A popular image in its day, Hunt's first religious painting was deceptively simple. Some of its symbolic details were later explained in a pamphlet written by the artist: "Physical light represented spiritual light—a lantern, the conservator of truth; rust, indicated the corrosion of the living faculties; weeds, the idle affections; a neglected orchard, the uncared for riches of God's garden; a bat which loveth darkness, ignorance; a blossoming thorn, the glorification from suffering—a crown, kingly power; the sacerdotal vestment, the priestly office etc."

G. F. WATTS, *FOR HE HAD GREAT POSSESSIONS*
1894, oil
Trustees of the Watts Gallery

The impact of this restrained composition derives as much from what the artist omits as from what he chooses to include. The rich young man hangs his head in dejection, having been told by Jesus that he must relinquish his wealth to gain eternal life. His "great possessions" are indicated only through his jeweled finger rings and the costly fur-trimmed robe that tantalizingly masks the young man's features.

Our modern word *parable* derives from the Greek word *parabole* (meaning "to cast alongside"), which in turn was a translation of the Hebrew term *mashal*. Both the Greek and the Hebrew expressions have much wider connotations than our generalized present-day usage, outlined above. The Hebrew *mashal* described a whole gamut of figurative language, embracing pithy, proverb-like sayings, prophetic utterances, taunts, questions, and riddles, as well as short narratives. Jesus' sayings (thirty of which the Gospels designate specifically as parables) are similarly diverse. The Parable of the Budding Fig Tree (Mt 24:32–36, Mk 13:28–32, Lk 21:29–33), for example, can be read as prophecy, while the rhetoric recorded by Mark 3:23–25 ("How can Satan cast out Satan?") qualifies as a riddle. In Luke 4:23 Jesus makes use of the proverb "Physician, heal thyself," as well as the laconic question (6:39) "Can the blind lead the blind? shall they not both fall into the ditch?" while the Gospel of Matthew (5:14) includes the utterance "Ye are the light of the world. A city that is set on a hill cannot be hid."

The parable was not an entirely novel concept for Jesus and his contemporaries, for Jesus was in fact adapting a genre that had already featured in several Old Testament books. Stories such as the parable of the eagles and the vine recounted by Ezekiel (17:2–10) and the song of the vineyard in Isaiah (5:1–7) were the antecedents of Jesus' parables. Only Nathan's parable to David about the poor man and the rich man (2 Sm, 12:1–10) is a true equivalent to Jesus' parable style; in the Old Testament story, David's judgmental condemnation of the rich man's lack of compassion is turned against him with Nathan's conclusion "Thou art the man"—just as Jesus used parables such as that of the Wicked Tenants to indict his audience.

Originating from the root verb *mshl* (probably meaning "to be like"), the Hebrew *mashal,* like its Greek counterpart *parabole,* relies on comparison and juxtaposition to make its point, and Jesus' parables, too, abound with such similitudes, his comparisons typically invoking everyday events—a crop being planted, bread making, accounts being settled, a coin misplaced—to describe the kingdom of heaven. Some comparisons were less explicit and drew instead upon metaphors familiar to the Jewish mind-set— for example, the visualization of God as a king or a householder, of the Israelites as his servants, or even the concept of the coming of his kingdom as a wedding.

The format which perhaps conforms most closely to the popular concept of parables are those stories that describe one-shot events, experienced by individuals, and examples of this type include the parables of the Wedding Feast, the Unjust Judge, and the Unmerciful Servant. Some of these particularized narratives (such as the Rich Man and Lazarus, the Unjust Steward, or the Good Samaritan) function as "example stories," providing a demonstration of appropriate behavior in a given situation. Other parables function by means of allegory, in which the story's various components carry an alternative meaning to that which is readily suggested, not always discernible without a "key." An allegorical reading of Matthew's Parable of the Wedding Feast, for example, might interpret the servants as prophets or apostles, the king as God, and the unwilling guests as the people of Israel. Some parables, notably those of the Sower and the Wheat and the Tares, are accompanied by their own built-in allegorical explanation, but these often raise more questions than they provide answers. As we shall see later, some scholars doubt the authenticity of such explanations, arguing that the technique is anachronistic and doesn't accord with Jesus' overall approach (his declared intention to "utter things which have been kept secret from the foundation of the world"); for others allegory is a legitimate component and one that Jesus, a skilled parabolist, would have wanted to incorporate into his teaching. Opinion is also divided on the number of Jesus' parables, and counts vary from about thirty to nearly double that figure (the latter taking a very broad view of what constitutes a parable and including short sayings and figures of speech).

Despite their apparent abundance, parables do not feature at all in the Gospel of Saint John or any other New Testament book and are recorded only in the Synoptic Gospels (so called because of the similarities of the three texts, which often read word for word when placed alongside one another in a "synopsis"). The Gospel of Saint Thomas, a collection of sayings attributed to Jesus discovered at Nag Hammadi in Egypt in 1945, also includes several of the parables found in the New Testament, but because this book is generally regarded as an independent source, one outside the traditional canon, it will not be referred to in this present study. The dense concentration of parables in the Synoptic Gospels indicates Jesus' reliance on them as a teaching aid, and it has been calculated that roughly one third of his teaching was effected through them; as Matthew suggests, "All these things spake Jesus unto the multitude; and without a parable spake he not unto them."

Helpful as the Gospelists' labeling of parables is for later readers, Jesus in his short career developed a distinctive style as a communicator, enabling his parables to be recognized by their own characteristics. The format of his parables reflects the needs of Jesus' original audience, who, as listeners rather than readers, didn't have the option we have today of consulting a written text to remind themselves of the story. One of the first things to strike contemporary readers is the concision of the parables; often containing his narrative within a single sentence or verse (as in the parables of the Mustard Seed and the Treasure in the Field), Jesus tells his audience exactly what they need to know in order to remember the story, and excludes any superfluous details that might cloud the issues. Increasingly aware as his mission unfolded that his time on earth would be limited, Jesus knew that brevity was also essential if he was to convey his message of repentance and salvation to as many people as possible. Much of this compression, running counter to modern literary trends, results from psychological detail being suppressed. No motive is offered as to why the Prodigal Son should suddenly demand his portion of the family inheritance and why he exiles himself so thoroughly from his family and native land, or why the Two Sons should both refuse to work in their father's vineyard and why one subsequently changes his mind; similarly in the Parable of the

Two Debtors, Jesus provides no explanation of how the first man—a lowly servant—has managed to run up the staggering debt of ten thousand talents, or what prompts him to attack his colleague so viciously. Such omissions, however, are selective and considerable detail is supplied when pertinent to the story. Figures are meticulously recorded in the parables—debts owing, talents left in trust, profits made, the hours at which laborers are hired, yields of wheat, and so on. Descriptive detail is used (albeit with the economy that an epigrammist would admire) to vivify the narrative—for example, the relative positions of the Rich Man and Lazarus are succinctly presented through their attire (the Rich Man wears purple and fine linen, while Lazarus' skin is clothed in sores licked by dogs) and their dining arrangements (the Rich Man enjoys lavish meals, while Lazarus scavenges for leftovers). In his account of the Parable of the Great Supper, Luke records the excuses of the recalcitrant guests in some detail—the feebleness of their protestations (their worldly preoccupations with their latest acquisitions of land, oxen, and matrimony) show how misplaced their priorities are. Such oscillations between detail and omission accelerate the narrative, enabling Jesus to rapidly reach the point of the parable, strategically placed at the end of his stories for maximum impact: "For I say unto you, that none of those men which were bidden shall taste of my supper."

Ever mindful of the need to hold his audience's attention, Jesus deployed in his parables the narrative techniques common to other forms of folk literature. As in fairy tales, several parables hinge around reversals of fortune, and often the most unlikely characters end up as beneficiaries of a happy ending—a profligate son is welcomed home, society's outcasts are invited to a lavish meal, even a tax collector succeeds in triumphing over a pious Pharisee in the repentance stakes. Repetition, too, plays a key role, acting as an *aide-mémoire* while propelling the plot. Thus we witness the succession of servants mistreated by the Wicked Tenants, a sequence culminating in the brutal murder of the landlord's beloved son, the last emissary to be sent out. So, too, in the Parable of the Laborers in the Vineyard, we are shown a stream of workers hired at different times of the day; we expect their wages to be commensurate with the hours they have worked, but the owner has other plans. Expectations are raised and then confounded—another form of reversal. Reiterated phrases also add to the narrative texture, as in the Parable of the Unforgiving Servant, where both debtors utter the same plea for mercy—"Have patience with me, and I will pay thee all"—but with drastically different outcomes. In Luke's Gospel a strand of repetition links several separate stories, as in the sequence of parables with the theme of "lost and found." All three parables—the

OVERLEAF: REMBRANDT VAN RYN, *THE 100 GUILDER PRINT*
c. 1649, etching, drypoint and burin
© British Museum

Lost Sheep, the Lost Coin, and the Prodigal Son—conclude by stressing the joy experienced at retrieving what was lost.

Jesus' parables also share the fairy tale's fondness for grouping events and characters—three servants entrusted with talents (Matthew), ten servants entrusted with pounds (Luke), two groups of five bridesmaids waiting to accompany the bridegroom to a wedding, two servants (one faithful, the other not), two debtors, two sons, and such groupings also help construct the comparisons inherent in parable format. The parables often treat these clusters of people as single entities and—Luke's Gospel excepted—the parables' *dramatis personae* tend to be sparsely drawn, often characterized by what others say about them: "O thou wicked servant!," "wise virgin," "thou fool." In contrast to this economy, Luke's parables and particularly those unique to his Gospel are peopled with vividly drawn characters in which we can easily recognize "real" individuals—the self-righteous but sulky older brother in the Prodigal Son, the persistent widow with nothing to lose, and the Rich Man whose feudal arrogance survives even death and the ignominy of hell. Focusing on events and situations, Jesus avoids describing what his characters look like—a shrewd omission contributing to the parables' universal appeal and encouraging the listener/reader to absorb the characters' response to the events at hand. The Gospelists themselves adopted this approach when they came to retell Christ's life, and Jesus' physical appearance went signally unremarked upon in their accounts.

The only narrator of parables in the New Testament, Jesus was challenged at first by his disciples for his use of them to teach largely uneducated crowds. When the disciples find themselves baffled by the hidden meanings of the Parable of the Sower, Matthew records their bewilderment ("Why speakest thou to them in parables?") and Jesus goes on to explain, "Unto you it is given to know the mysteries of the kingdom of God: but to others in parables; that seeing they might not see, and hearing they might not understand." Luke's version of Jesus' response (quoted here) is in fact the most succinct of the three Gospelists, but all three seem to invoke the idea of parables as mysterious speech. Mark's Gospel in particular emphasizes the idea of mystery, a feature that has been ascribed to his theory that Jesus was not recognized as the Messiah ("the anointed one") because he concealed his true status. In this theory of the "messianic secret," it follows that Jesus would not want the parables to be easily deciphered. Matthew employs a similar paradox but additionally invokes the idea of the parables as the outcome of ancient prophecy ("And in them is fulfilled the prophecy of Esaias") and Jesus' response is indeed reminiscent of God's words to the prophet Isaiah: "Go, and tell this people, Hear ye indeed, but understand not; and see ye indeed, but perceive not. Make the heart of this people fat, and make their ears heavy, and shut their eyes, lest they see with their eyes, and hear with their ears, and understand with their heart, and convert and be healed."

All three Synoptics record Jesus' distinction between the incomprehension and spiritual deafness of the crowds and the privileged understanding and insight of the disciples: "But blessed are your eyes, for they see: and your ears, for they hear" (Matthew). The apparent contradictions of Jesus' explanation tie in with the story of the Sower, itself a parable about different levels of hearing and understanding. Nevertheless, Jesus' riddling remarks have been interpreted in a number of ways; for some their echoes of Old Testament writers such as Isaiah and Jeremiah link the parable to long-standing prophecies relating to the obduracy of Israel and the disasters that would ensue, while others read the inscrutability of the parable as a ploy by Jesus to make his audience work hard toward an understanding of the Kingdom of Heaven, in that their efforts puzzling over the parables would be rewarded by a more profound knowledge. The distinction Jesus drew between the understanding of the crowds and that of his disciples is, however, somewhat contradicted by the latter's initial failure to grasp Jesus' meaning in the Parable of the Sower and, subsequently, the Parable of the Wheat and the Tares: "Declare unto us the parable of the tares of the field." Mark's Gospel is particularly unsparing of the disciples' travails, and in his account of events Jesus seems surprised by their response: "Know ye not this parable? and how then will ye know all parables?" Mark, too, notes the "extra coaching" they receive: "And when they were alone, he explained all things to his disciples." Nevertheless, the disciples' ability does develop as the story of Jesus' mission unfolds and such references fade from the text.

But Jesus' parables were not only addressed to crowds, eager to hear him speak, to witness miracles and receive healing, they were also addressed to his opponents, people who questioned his authority, as well as his methods and motives. Jesus soon fell foul of the religious establishment of the day—the chief priests and elders of the temple—and the two main Jewish religious parties, the Sadducees and the Pharisees. A lay movement, Pharisaism placed great emphasis on the strict observance of the religious laws (as elucidated by their scribes following a tradition of oral interpretation) and had risen to prominence since its inception in the second century B.C. The Sadducees, which in Jesus' time were the majority party on the Sanhedrin (parliamentary judicial council), were the more conservative of the two parties; while their faith was based on the written tradition of the law, they were equally strict in their adherence to it. Much of Jesus' teaching ran counter to the Sadducees' and Pharisees' exacting understanding of the law, but Jesus made clear he was not trying to gainsay the law ("For verily I say unto you, Till heaven and earth pass, one jot or tittle shall in no wise pass from the law, till all be fulfilled"). Rather, he taught that the spirit of the law should be observed as well as the letter, as, for example, in his advice to the law-abiding young man who wanted to attain eternal life to sell everything and give his possessions to the poor. Such a requirement was not strictly speaking a tenet of the law, but it was an extension of its original (increasingly neglected) directive that the rich should make provision for the poor. Jesus taught that the observance of the law should not be so inflexible as to ignore God's overall intentions, and he put his words into practice both by allowing his disciples to pick some ears of corn to assuage their hunger on the Sabbath, and by himself healing the sick on that divinely ordained day of rest.

Such teaching was interpreted as a threat to the supremacy of the religious elite, and the Gospels record several occasions of the antagonism Jesus provoked. Both the Sadducees and Pharisees tried to trap Jesus by asking him contentious legal questions —about divorce, life after death, the necessity of paying taxes to Rome—and Jesus was criticized for breaking the Sabbath and for associating with sinners and other despised elements of society. Accordingly, several parables were addressed specifically to the Pharisees, with Jesus countering their criticisms while offering a few of his own. Parables such as the Wicked Tenants explicitly criticized the failure of the religious elite to safeguard the spiritual well-being of Israel in accordance with God's wishes, a barb that evidently hit home but engendered not repentance but this fateful response: "And the chief priests and scribes the same hour sought to lay hands on him and they feared the people: for they perceived that he had spoken this parable against them." The parables of the Wedding Feast, the Talents/Pounds, and the Two Debtors are also in this vein; the Parable of the Good Samaritan responds to the questioning of an individual temple lawyer ("And who is my neighbor?"), while Luke's Parable of the Great Supper follows a Pharisee's overly pious exclamation during a meal at which Jesus was a fellow guest, "Blessed is he that shall eat bread in the kingdom of God."

Some discrepancies do, however, exist between the Gospels as to whom parables were spoken and where they were placed in the chronology. In Matthew the Parable of the Lost Sheep is prompted by the disciples' question "Who is the greatest in the kingdom of heaven?" His concept of the solitary lost sheep demonstrated the importance of the "little ones" in God's kingdom and emphasized the diligence of the search needed to find them. Luke, however, placed the parable as a response to the clerics' criticism "And the Pharisees and scribes murmured saying, This man receiveth sinners, and eateth with them." This version, although verbally similar to Matthew's, reiterates the prerequisite of repentance in God's kingdom and stresses the joy with which repentant sinners are received there. Such textual differences probably arose in part because of the increasingly fragmentary nature of the oral tradition, and in part, too, because of the changing needs of the early Church; confrontational in format, many parables would

---

THE GOOD SAMARITAN
(DETAIL FROM WINDOW AT CHARTRES CATHEDRAL)
c. 1210, stained glass
Photo: Copyright Sonia Halliday and Laura Lushington

"But a certain Samaritan, as he journeyed, came to where he was: and when he saw him, he had compassion on him, and went to him, and bound up his wounds, pouring in oil and wine, and set him on his own beast, and brought him to an inn, and took care of him."

JAN SANDERS VAN HEMESSEN, *THE PARABLE OF THE UNMERCIFUL SERVANT*
c. 1548–52, oil on panel
University of Michigan Museum of Art, 1959/1.108

With an ambiguity reminiscent of the parables themselves, van Hemessen's multilayered composition is open to a number of interpretations. Is the figure being led off to jail in the background the Unmerciful Servant receiving his punishment, or is it the fellow servant he so cruelly mistreats? Is the disdainful figure in the left foreground the Unmerciful Servant demanding his colleague to repay him, or is it his master condemning him to be "delivered . . . to the tormentors"?

have originally been aimed at opponents, but as the Church grew, the need for justification diminished and some adjustments were necessary to cater to a community who were already believers and who took Jesus' authority as a given.

Leaving aside the question of the evolution of his audiences, some of Jesus' intentions can perhaps be discerned more readily through the themes he explored in his parables. Many of Jesus' parables discuss the kingdom of heaven ("Whereunto shall we liken the kingdom of God? or with what comparison shall we compare it?"), and the concept of God's kingdom was one central to Jewish belief. Traditionally, the coming of the kingdom signaled the fulfillment of God's promise to the Israelites after their exodus from Egypt that they would be first among nations if they kept his laws: "If ye will obey my voice indeed, and keep my covenant, then ye shall be a peculiar treasure unto me above all people." As Israel's sufferings continued, however, the longed-for realization of God's Covenant remained remote and increasingly became envisaged as a supernatural event, no lesser one in fact than the end of the world itself. At the Day of Judgment God would punish sinners and reward the righteous—that is, the Jewish people—accepting them into his kingdom and thus effecting their triumph over other nations. Matthew's Gospel particularly chronicles this aspect of Jesus' teaching, and virtually the whole of his thirteenth chapter is occupied by parables about the kingdom. In contrast to Mark and his belief in the "messianic secret," Matthew's Jesus seems overwhelmingly concerned with helping his audience understand the nature of this mysterious realm and, in a series of parables about watching and waiting, alerting them to its potentially imminent arrival. Perhaps the real impact of these parables, however, lies in the importance they attach to the relationship between individuals' behavior and their acceptance into the kingdom. Acting as "spiritual wake-up calls," parables such as the Thief in the Night and the Wise and Foolish Virgins urge listeners to be prepared for the kingdom, and to conduct themselves appropriately (by keeping God's laws) while waiting for it. Several of the parables, such as the Friend at Midnight and the Importunate Widow, imply that the wait for the kingdom might indeed be long and dangerous and offer examples of fortitude, faith, and prayer as encouragement.

Neither did Jesus shrink from describing the finality of the Last Judgment, God's unshakeable resolve and steely justice being demonstrated in no uncertain terms in parables such as the Wheat and Tares, the Dragnet, the Talents/Pounds, and the Rich Man and Lazarus. Parables such as the Unjust Debtor, the Prodigal Son, the Good Samaritan, and Luke's Parable of the Wedding Guest also provide models of suitable behavior required by God—repentance, forgiveness, compassion, and humility are all shown to be necessary attributes for entry into his kingdom. Other parables, notably those of the Wicked Tenants and the Talents, with their theme of betrayal, criticize the Pharisees' behavior, offering a negative exemplum of conduct to be avoided. Continuing the theme of spiritual deafness found in the Old Testament, parables such as the Sower, the Hidden Treasure, and the Pearl of Great Price teach the importance of not only hearing God's word but of understanding it and acting upon it (the latter two parables also suggestive of the speed with which a suitable response should be effected). For some, Jesus' mission fulfilled the prophecies of Scripture and represented this long-anticipated arrival of the kingdom of heaven, an event heralded by Jesus' forerunner, John the Baptist, "the voice in the wilderness." In other quarters, Jesus seemed an impostor and blasphemer, a Galilean peasant with no apparent formal religious training, a troublemaker who questioned the accepted mores of the day. By any standards, however, Jesus' career precipitated a decisive stand-off between the old order and a new, emerging state of things, as indicated by his parables of the Wine Bottles and the Garments.

These themes, expressed here in very general terms, articulate the underlying concerns of Jesus' parables. A number of factors contribute to the continuing debate that surrounds attempts to offer definitive interpretations of parables individually and as a whole. The time lag between oral and written transmission, the coexistence of three overlapping but distinct Gospels, and the rich seam of allusion and textual ambiguities—all have contributed to the parables' controversial status among their interpreters. The Gospelists themselves can be counted among this group, being the parables' first written expositors, as theirs was a task that involved translating the original spoken Aramaic into Greek. Writing after Jesus' lifetime, they were not, however, entirely disinterested chroniclers of his career, and each had his own motives, approach, and target audience. While the dating of the Gospels remains controversial, Mark's is widely acknowledged to have been the first text (perhaps written A.D. 65–75), followed by Matthew and then Luke. Luke is thought to have composed his text as late as the second century A.D., and his Gospel reflects the concerns of the early Church and takes a reconciliatory approach, stressing the universalism of Jesus' mission ("and that repentance and remission of sins should be preached in his name among all nations, beginning at Jerusalem") and reassuring both Jews and Gentiles of their place in the kingdom of heaven. The Good Samaritan and Prodigal Son are parables exclusive to Luke's Gospel and are significant for their humanity and emphasis on forgiveness. Commentators have also noted the wealth of domestic details and vividly drawn characters in Luke's parables, as well as their portrayal of Jesus' social interaction with both sinners and righteous alike and his interest in helping the dispossessed elements of his society— women, children, the poor, the ill, the disabled. Mark and Matthew, writing in the century of Christ's death, have bloodier axes to grind, new converts to keep in order, and confused loyalties to untangle. Mark's sympathies seem to be Gentile, and his explanation of Palestinian customs and his view of the wide-ranging mission to be undertaken by the disciples infer a non-Jewish audience. His text—the shortest of all the Gospels and the first to attempt a chronological account of Jesus' life—is primarily concerned with recording significant events of Jesus' life rather than discourse and so contains few parables. In contrast, Matthew's Gospel reflects the outlook of Jewish Christianity; in his account Jesus only expects to look after the "lost sheep of Israel," and his life is seen in the context of Old Testament expectations. Matthew's and Mark's Gospels are characterized by their apocalyptic interest; both incline toward a pessimistic worldview, similar to that of Old Testament writers Ezekiel and Daniel, and their parables of the Wicked Tenants and the Unjust Debtor (a.k.a. Unforgiving Servant) became uncompromising tales of treachery and retribution. Mark's Gospel in particular makes numerous references to suffering, which are believed to allude to the persecutions of the emperor Nero's reign; thus his has earned the sobriquet the "Martyr Gospel."

Subsequent interpreters have enriched the debate, like the Synoptic writers themselves, bringing the preoccupations of their age to their study. It is a measure of the robust richness of the parables that they have withstood such scrutiny and continue to admit new interpretational possibilities. From the period of the early Church up until the last century, allegorization was the prevalent approach to textual interpretation. Early commentators such as Philo of Alexandria, writing in the first century A.D., and Origen, in the third century A.D., followed the New Testament writers in allegorizing

HONORÉ DAUMIER, *THE GOOD SAMARITAN*
nineteenth century, oil on canvas
Glasgow Museums, the Burrell Collection

Daumier's broadly worked painting unsentimentally describes the cumbersome—almost comic—progress of the Samaritan and his patient as they make their way to the inn.

the parables but often outdid them by finding hidden subtext in even the smallest details of the narrative. Saint Augustine, writing in the fourth and fifth centuries A.D., provided an interpretation of the Good Samaritan in the same vein, detecting a theological meaning in every element of the story. Thus the robbers represented the devil; their victim, left for dead on the Jericho-Jerusalem road, represented Adam; the innkeeper was the Apostle Paul, while the compassionate Samaritan was Christ himself. The dominance of allegory in medieval thinking was discussed by C. S. Lewis in his book *The Allegory of Love* (1936), and a decade later E. Auerbach wrote that at the end of the Middle Ages "every kind of serious realism was in danger of being choked to death by the vines of allegory."

Allegory, however, has never been universally acclaimed, and Saint John Chrysostom counseled a different approach to that of his contemporary Saint Augustine: "Interpret the elements in the parables that are urgent and essential . . . do not waste time on all the details . . . Seek out the scope for which the parable was designed and be not overbusy with the rest." The Reformation in the sixteenth century also witnessed a decline in allegory's popularity, with both John Calvin and Martin Luther being opposed to its methods and its proponents (derided by Luther as "clerical jugglers performing monkey tricks"). In spite of such opposition, Luther was unable to completely resist allegorization, as his sermon on the Good Samaritan demonstrates.

Allegory's long reign over the parables continued largely unchecked by such dissent until the end of the nineteenth century, when its longevity was finally halted by the work of German scholar Alfred Jülicher. Published just before the turn of the century, his ground-breaking study, *Die Gleichnisreden Jesu* (The Parables of Jesus), presented parables not as allegories but rather as simple stories making a single moral point. Jülicher refuted the concept of Jesus as an allegorist, instead proposing that the allegorical elements were later additions provided by the Evangelists. Jülicher's approach was radical and influential. Most subsequent commentators accepted his rejection of allegory but were quick to disagree with his theory of a single point, critical of the way that this approach, like allegory itself, robbed the text of its potential multiple meanings.

The twentieth century has witnessed the emergence of many different and often conflicting approaches in parable studies. The British scholar C. H. Dodd agreed with Jülicher's antiallegorical stance but led some commentators down another avenue with his proposal that the parables should be examined in relation to their historical setting. Dodd's approach also stressed the parables' eschatological context (that is, their relationship to Jewish beliefs about the end of the world). For Dodd, Jesus' ministry was evidence that the kingdom of heaven had already arrived and, accordingly, the parables were not predictions of a future event but commentaries on the present. Dodd coined the phrase "realized eschatology" to describe this theory, but his views, too, have been modified, challenged, or refuted. Joachim Jeremias, a German theologian, while sharing Dodd's concern for the historicity of the parables, saw them (rather more cautiously) as a stage of the ongoing establishment of God's kingdom—in other words, eschatology in the process of being fully realized. Having spent his youth in Palestine, Jeremias was able to use his extensive knowledge of the locale and its customs in his attempt to establish the precise historical and cultural background of the parables and, by removing what he deemed to be later additions, to study them in their "original form."

Parable interpretation has also become influenced by the existentialist and structuralist theories prevalent in other disciplines. Interest in the parable as an independent literary object grew as credence in the overtly historical approach waned. The roles of metaphor and symbol within Jesus' parables have been scrutinized, notably in the work of Amos Wilder and Robert Funk. Instead of being seen purely as historical events, the parables have increasingly come to be viewed as "language events" whose forceful narratives appeal directly to the imagination to communicate the transcendent reality of the kingdom of heaven. In complete rejection of Jülicher's theories, modern scholars have acknowledged the open-ended nature of many parables and their ability to carry several meanings simultaneously. In a less introspective vein, Jesus' stories have been studied in the context of other parables from different traditions—for example, the rabbinic parables that developed after Jesus' lifetime.

The increasingly literary stance adopted by critics and their validation of parables as literature, while broadening the parameters of research, also acknowledges (somewhat belatedly) what writers and artists have understood for generations. Vigorous and individual, the parable, like any respected art form, has proved itself capable of nourishing other works of art and providing inspiration for artists in many media. In literature their influence has been pervasive, manifesting itself either as allusions to specific parables or through imitation of the biblical parabolic form. The compelling narratives, dramatic scenarios, and moral content of the parables have proved of particular service to playwrights. The sixteenth and seventeenth centuries in Europe witnessed a striking vogue for plays based on the Prodigal Son, and Shakespeare's oeuvre contains numerous parable references. More recently the themes and formats of the parables have inspired dramatists like Bertolt Brecht (who described his plays as "parables for the theater"), Samuel Beckett, and the South African playwright Athol Fugard, whose play *A Place with the Pigs* recounts the fluctuating fortunes of a prodigal son within a communist system.

Writers as diverse as Chaucer, John Bunyan, Charles Dickens, George Eliot, and Graham Greene have all used the parables in their own work. Pearl in Hawthorne's *The Scarlet Letter* can be read as a reference to the "pearl of great price," and both Daniel Defoe's famous castaway and James Joyce's Stephen Daedalus each identifies himself as a prodigal son at various points in the narratives of *Robinson Crusoe* and *Ulysses,* respectively. The work of metaphysical poet George Herbert shares the beguiling simplicity of the parables, as well as their use of the familiar and domestic, to convey mysterious, spiritual truths; more explicitly, his poem "The Pearl" refers to Matthew's Parable of the Pearl of Great Price ("I flie to thee, and fully understand/Both the main sale, and the

BARTOLOMÉ ESTEBAN MURILLO, *THE RETURN OF THE PRODIGAL SON*
1667/1670, oil on canvas
National Gallery of Art, Washington, Gift of the Avalon Foundation, © 1996 Board of Trustees

Murillo's picturesque paintings of street urchins were as sought after as his devotional works. Here two smiling children share in the tender family reconciliation. In one especially lighthearted touch, the household's pet dog rushes up to the returned prodigal in excited recognition.

commodities;/And at what rate and price I have thy love"). In this century the poet William Plomer provided the librettos for Benjamin Britten's *Three Parables for Church Performance,* which included one on the Prodigal Son, and, remaining in the world of twentieth-century music, Vincent Persichetti composed a series of "parables" for different musical instruments. The theme of the Prodigal Son also provided inspiration for Prokofiev's ballet of the same title (designs for which were executed by artist and filmmaker Derek Jarman as a project while studying at the Slade School of Fine Art, London). In modern fiction, parables have been particularly associated with the work of Franz Kafka—his stark narratives have been described by the South American writer Jorge Luis Borges (himself often regarded as a parabolist) as "a parable or series of parables on the theme of the moral relationship of the individual with his God and with his God's incomprehensible universe."

The urge to translate parables into tangible images seems to have been irrepressible throughout history, and Jesus' narratives have adapted readily to the demands of the visual arts. In applied art the parables have even been considered appropriate subject matter for domestic objects destined for daily use—a neat reference perhaps to the often mundane nature of Jesus' similitudes. The Wallace Collection in London houses a brightly glazed earthenware stove tile, dated 1572 and of German origin, which depicts the Prodigal Son embracing a prostitute. In the same collection, a ceramic flask of slightly earlier date is decorated on its several sides with scenes from the Parable of the Rich Man and Lazarus—a cautionary tale intended to give its user pause for thought? The didactic import of the parables made them a logical choice for church decoration, when prior to the advent of widespread literacy, visual images helped convey the teaching of Bible and the preacher. A window in the South Aisle at Chartres Cathedral containing a stained-glass portrayal of the Good Samaritan serves just such a purpose— literally enlightening the congregation of this story. The impact of Jesus' narratives has also been realized three-dimensionally in sculpture, and the Lithuanian Jewish émigré artist Jacques Lipchitz modeled the Prodigal Son in bronze as part of the exploration of religious themes that characterized his later career. As the images reproduced here testify, the parables have endowed painters and draughtsmen in particular with a rich legacy. The second part of this book will explore in more detail how artists through the centuries have responded to the parables and the relationship between these works and Christian art as a whole.

Extraordinarily resonant aspects of the New Testament, for many of us the parables enter our consciousness at an early age. Translating readily from the mountains and lakesides of Galilee to classrooms and churches the world over, stories such as the Good Samaritan, the Prodigal Son, and the Unjust Debtor continue to teach the principles of Christian belief and behavior. As their longevity and popularity indicate, the parables also reveal fundamental truths about ourselves and about humanity itself, and they remain an abiding influence in the world today.

THE PARABLE OF THE WISE AND FOOLISH BUILDERS

❧

MATTHEW 7:24–27

Therefore whosoever heareth these sayings of mine, and doeth them, I will liken him unto a wise man, which built his house upon a rock:

And the rain descended, and the floods came, and the winds blew, and beat upon that house; and it fell not: for it was founded upon a rock.

And every one that heareth these sayings of mine, and doeth them not, shall be likened unto a foolish man, which built his house upon the sand:

And the rain descended, and the floods came, and the winds blew, and beat upon that house; and it fell: and great was the fall of it.

LUKE 6:47–49

Whosoever cometh to me, and heareth my sayings, and doeth them, I will shew you to whom he is like:

He is like a man which built an house, and digged deep, and laid the foun-

WORKSHOP OF DOMENICO FETTI,
THE PARABLE OF THE RICH MAN AND LAZARUS
1618/1628, oil on panel
National Gallery of Art, Washington, Samuel H. Kress Collection, © 1997 Board of Trustees

dation on a rock: and when the flood arose, the stream beat vehemently upon that house, and could not shake it: for it was founded upon a rock.

But he that heareth, and doeth not, is like a man that without a foundation built an house upon the earth; against which the stream did beat vehemently, and immediately it fell; and the ruin of the house was great.

COMMENTARY

Coming at the end of the Sermon on the Mount (on a plain, in Luke's version), this parable underlines the dual importance of listening to and acting on God's words. The parable restates, in figurative language, the point made by Jesus moments earlier: "Not every one that saith unto me, Lord, Lord, shall enter into the kingdom of heaven; but he that doeth the will of my Father which is in Heaven."

Jesus warns against empty spiritual gestures, comparing two builders whose houses are both tested by storms. Here, however, the similarities end and the audience's attention is drawn instead to the different building techniques used by the men and the ensuing consequences. The storm is a vivid image of the Last Judgment; bearing down on both houses with equal ferocity, it tests their foundations to the utmost. The explicit designation of the men as "wise" and "foolish" (in Matthew's version) prevents the audience from forming their own conclusions, in contrast to other parables that provoke thought and demand an opinion. In this instance Jesus prefers to leave his listeners in no doubt as to which man deserves to enter the kingdom of heaven.

Compact in format, the parable is nevertheless rich in allusions. Although the builders are the ostensible subjects of the parable, it is their houses that form the central image. A familiar metaphor for the Church (in the sense both of a building and a community), the house built on rock recalls Jesus' charge to the disciple Peter, recorded by Matthew later in his Gospel, "Thou art Peter, and upon this rock I will build my church." The resilience of the wise man's house also contains echoes of Noah, another man who built prudently in the face of a deluge, while the great fall of the house built on sand evokes the destruction of the Temple in Jerusalem in A.D. 70.

Jesus concludes the parable on a pessimistic note, stressing the utter collapse of the house built on sand, and Matthew records the audience's astonished reaction to Jesus' teaching style, "For he taught them as one having authority, and not as the scribes."

THE PARABLE OF THE OLD AND NEW GARMENTS

MATTHEW 9:16

No man putteth a piece of new cloth unto an old garment, for that which is put in to fill it up taketh from the garment, and the rent is made worse.

MARK 2:21

No man also seweth a piece of new cloth on an old garment: else the new piece that filled it up taketh away from the old, and the rent is made worse.

LUKE 5:36

And he spake also a parable unto them; No man putteth a piece of a new garment upon an old; if otherwise, then both the new maketh a rent, and the piece that was taken out of the new agreeth not with the old.

THE PARABLE OF THE OLD AND NEW WINE BOTTLES

MATTHEW 9:17

Neither do men put new wine into old bottles: else the bottles break, and the wine runneth out, and the bottles perish: but they put new wine into new bottles, and both are preserved.

MARK 2:22

And no man putteth new wine into old bottles: else the new wine doth burst the bottles, and the wine is spilled, and the bottles will be marred: but new wine must be put into new bottles.

LUKE 5:37–39

And no man putteth new wine into old bottles; else the new wine will burst the bottles, and be spilled, and the bottles shall perish.

But new wine must be put into new bottles; and both are preserved.

No man also having drunk old wine straightway desireth new: for he saith, The old is better.

This pair of parables, common to all the Synoptic Gospels, was used by Jesus to illustrate the differences between his mission and that of his predecessors. Using the mundane domestic activities of mending clothes and bottling wine, Jesus demonstrated the incompatibility of the old and new religious orders, in spite of their outward similarities.

Some variations between the three versions are discernible, indicative of the evolving early tradition and reflecting the preoccupations of the individual authors. Matthew's approach is more conciliatory than Mark's and envisages the survival of both old and new; Luke's version tends toward Matthew's in tone but, contrarily, adds a line in which the old wine is preferred to the new. Luke's meaning becomes clearer if this line is read as an ironic comment on mankind's habitual resistance to innovation and change—an attitude Jesus knew only too well.

The opposition of new wine against old is particularly resonant for Christians, used to associating wine with Jesus' blood, following Jesus' words to his disciples at the Last Supper, "And he took the cup, and when he had given thanks, he gave it to them: and they all drank of it./And he said unto them, This is my blood of the new testament, which is shed for many,/Verily I say unto you, I will drink no more fruit of the vine, until that day that I drink it new in the kingdom of God" (Mark 14:23–25).

THE PARABLE OF THE SOWER AND JESUS' EXPLANATION

MATTHEW 13:1–9

The same day went Jesus out of the house, and sat by the sea side.

And great multitudes were gathered together unto him, so that he went into a ship, and sat; and the whole multitude stood on the shore.

And he spake many things unto them in parables, saying, Behold, a sower went forth to sow;

And when he sowed, some seeds fell by the way side, and the fowls came and devoured them up:

SIR JOHN EVERETT MILLAIS, *THE PARABLE OF THE SOWER*
1864, wood engraving

Millais's engraving focuses on the seed rather than the Sower, in an accurate rendition of the original parable. The artist wrote of this work, "I have made it landscape for variety, and to show the stony ground, briars, nettles, and fowls of the air, feeding upon the stray seed. The Sower who is supposed to have sown the side of the field is subordinate."

Some fell upon stony places, where they had not much earth: and forthwith they sprung up, because they had no deepness of earth:

And when the sun was up, they were scorched; and because they had no root, they withered away.

And some fell among thorns; and the thorns sprung up, and choked them:

But other fell into good ground, and brought forth fruit, some an hundredfold, some sixtyfold, some thirtyfold.

Who hath ears to hear, let him hear.

MATTHEW 13:18–23

Hear ye therefore the parable of the sower.

When any one heareth the word of the kingdom, and understandeth it not, then cometh the wicked one, and catcheth away that which was sown in his heart. This is he which received seed by the way side.

But he that received the seed into stony places, the same is he that heareth the word, and anon with joy receiveth it;

Yet hath he not root in himself, but dureth for a while: for when tribulation or persecution ariseth because of the word, by and by he is offended.

He also that received seed among the thorns is he that heareth the word; and the cares of this world, and the deceitfulness of riches, choke the word, and he becometh unfruitful.

But he that received seed into the good ground is he that heareth the word, and understandeth it; which also beareth fruit, and bringeth forth, some an hundredfold, some sixty, some thirty.

MARK 4:3–9

Hearken; Behold, there went out a sower to sow:

And it came to pass, as he sowed, some fell by the way side, and the fowls of the air came and devoured it up.

And some fell on stony ground, where it had not much earth; and immediately it sprang up, because it had no depth of earth:

But when the sun was up, it was scorched; and because it had no root, it withered away.

And some fell among thorns, and the thorns grew up, and choked it, and it yielded no fruit.

And other fell on good ground, and did yield fruit that sprang up and increased; and brought forth, some thirty, and some sixty, and some an hundred.

And he said unto them, He that hath ears to hear, let him hear.

And he said unto them, Know ye not this parable? and how then will ye know all parables?

The sower soweth the word.

And these are they by the way side, where the word is sown; but when they have heard, Satan cometh immediately, and taketh away the word that was sown in their hearts.

And these are they likewise which are sown on stony ground; who, when they have heard the word, immediately receive it with gladness;

And have no root in themselves, and so endure but for a time: afterward, when affliction or persecution ariseth for the word's sake, immediately they are offended.

And these are they which are sown among thorns; such as hear the word,

And the cares of this world, and the deceitfulness of riches, and the lusts of other things entering in, choke the word, and it becometh unfruitful.

And these are they which are sown on good ground; such as hear the word, and receive it, and bring forth fruit, some thirtyfold, some sixty, and some an hundred.

LUKE 8:4–8

And when much people were gathered together, and were come to him out of every city, he spake by a parable:

A sower went out to sow his seed: and as he sowed, some fell by the way side; and it was trodden down, and the fowls of the air devoured it.

And some fell upon a rock; and as soon as it was sprung up, it withered away, because it lacked moisture.

And some fell among thorns; and the thorns sprang up with it, and choked it.

And other fell on good ground, and sprang up, and bare fruit an hundredfold. And when he had said these things, he cried, He that hath ears to hear, let him hear.

LUKE 8:11–15

Now the parable is this: The seed is the word of God.

Those by the way side are they that hear; then cometh the devil, and taketh away the word out of their hearts, lest they should believe and be saved.

They on the rock are they, which when they hear, receive the word with joy; and these have no root, which for a while believe, and in time of temptation fall away.

VIATOR;

And that which fell among thorns are they, which when they have heard, go forth, and are choked with cares and riches and pleasures of this life, and bring no fruit to perfection.

But that on the good ground are they, which in an honest and good heart, having heard the word, keep it, and bring forth fruit with patience.

COMMENTARY

Perhaps the best known of the parables, the Sower is also one of the most important, and not only deals with the necessity of hearing God's word but also raises the issue of why Jesus chose to use parables for his teaching. The Gospels note that a large crowd had gathered to hear Jesus speak, but while their reaction to the parable is not recorded, Matthew does not conceal the disciples' consternation: "Why speakest thou unto them in parables?" In Mark's and Luke's versions of the event the disciples' own incomprehension is evident, Luke noting, "And his disciples asked him, saying, What might this parable be?" Before going on to explain the parable, Jesus reveals why he uses parables, although his response at first seems elusive and paradoxical:

Unto you it is given to know the mystery of the kingdom of God: but unto them that are without, all these things are done in parables:/That seeing they may see, and not perceive; and hearing they may hear, and not understand; lest at any time they should be converted, and their sins should be forgiven them.

Jesus emphasizes the disciples' special insight into the kingdom, as well as the mysterious nature of the kingdom, and contrasts it with the spiritual deafness of the crowds he teaches. Unreceptivity to God's word was not, however, a new phenomenon, and Jesus' words paraphrase almost exactly Old Testament Scriptures such as Isaiah (6:9–10):

And he said, go and tell this people, Hear ye indeed, but understand not; and see ye indeed, but perceive not. Make the heart of this people fat, and make

THE SOWER AMONG THORNS AND ON GOOD GROUND,
CANTERBURY CATHEDRAL
twelfth century, stained glass
Photo: Copyright Sonia Halliday and Laura Lushington

A stream of seed flowing from his hand, the Sower strides along the plowed field. Thorns spring up in places to consume the seed, but the grain also falls on good ground. In the foreground lies the Sower's crumpled cloak—cast off in the heat of the day—and in the background a hilly wooded landscape completes the pastoral scene.

their ears heavy, and shut their eyes, let they see with their eyes, and hear with their ears, and understand with their heart, and convert and be healed.

And Jeremiah (5:21):

Hear now this, O foolish people, and without understanding, which have eyes, and see not; which have ears, and hear not.

In this case, however, Jesus obliges his disciples and provides an allegorical explanation for the parable, in which each element of the story stands for something else—for example, "The seed is the word of God." An apparently agricultural anecdote, the Sower in fact catalogs the potential trials facing those who encounter the Word but ends on an upbeat note, the stupendous yield from a single grain of wheat suggesting the positive benefits of listening to God. While Jesus' stress on hearing and responding to the Word remains as vital today as it was for his original audience, for early Christians, often persecuted for their faith, the parable's allegory of the seed on stony ground must have had particular relevance.

Some commentators regard the explanation as an anachronism, viewing allegory as a later method of parable interpretation (and indeed it was a methodology that prevailed until the end of the nineteenth century). However, the allegory fits the parable snugly, and its propriety is further reinforced by the perception that elements of the Sower comment on subsequent events within the Gospel themselves. Thus, the seed which has no roots and which falls away in times of tribulation can also be seen as a foretaste of Jesus' desertion by his disciples in the Garden of Olives, as well as his desertion by the crowds in front of Pilate, while the seed sown among thorns, terrorized by "the cares of riches," effectively dramatizes the incident of the wealthy young man eager for eternal life whose riches Jesus urges him to abandon.

THE PARABLE OF THE WHEAT AND THE TARES AND JESUS' EXPLANATION

MATTHEW 13:24–30

Another parable put he forth unto them, saying, The kingdom of heaven is likened unto a man which sowed good seed in his field:

But while men slept, his enemy came and sowed tares among the wheat, and went his way.

But when the blade was sprung up, and brought forth fruit, then appeared the tares also.

ABRAHAM BLOEMAERT, *THE PARABLE OF THE TARES*
1624, oil on canvas
The Walters Art Gallery, Baltimore

ॐ

A seemingly idyllic rustic scene, Bloemaert's painting yields more sinister meanings on closer inspection. A group of farmworkers seem to be taking a well-earned siesta, although the picnic basket and empty earthenware pitcher hint that they might be sleeping off an overindulgent lunch. A naked couple slumber in the foreground, while a goat, symbolic of lust, stares knowingly at the viewer. While the workers sleep, another figure with horns and a tail—the devil—is busy contaminating the field in the background with weeds. During the Counter-Reformation period this parable was used to warn against the dissemination of heretical doctrines.

So the servants of the householder came and said unto him, Sir, didst not thou sow good seed in thy field? from whence then hath it tares?

He said unto them, An enemy hath done this. The servants said unto him, Wilt thou then that we go and gather them up?

But he said, Nay; lest while ye gather up the tares, ye root up also the wheat with them.

Let both grow together until the harvest: and in the time of harvest I will say to the reapers, Gather ye together first the tares, and bind them in bundles to burn them: but gather the wheat into my barn.

MATTHEW 13:36–43

Then Jesus sent the multitude away, and went into the house: and his disciples came unto him, saying, Declare unto us the parables of the tares in the field.

He answered and said unto them, He that soweth the good seed is the Son of man;

The field is the world; the good seed are the children of the kingdom; but the tares are the children of the wicked one;

The enemy that sowed them is the devil; the harvest is the end of the world; and the reapers are the angels.

As therefore the tares are gathered and burned in the fire; so shall it be in the end of this world.

The Son of man shall send forth his angels, and they shall gather out of his kingdom all things that offend, and them which do iniquity;

And shall cast them into a furnace of fire: there shall be wailing and gnashing of teeth.

Then shall the righteous shine forth as the sun in the kingdom of their Father. Who hath ears to hear, let him hear.

COMMENTARY

Having explained the Parable of the Sower, Jesus launches immediately into another parable, locating it in a similar agricultural milieu. As in the previous parable, the growth of the seed is jeopardized, although not by nature but by the malevolent action of an outside agency, "an enemy." The survival of the wheat is, however, ensured by the farmer's sensible strategy of allowing both wheat and weed to grow together and waiting until harvest to separate them. Other parables of growth—those of the Mustard Seed and the Leaven—follow in quick succession before Jesus dismisses the crowd and the disciples can again demand of him, "Declare unto us the parable of the tares of the field." Although the Parable of the Sower must have suggested possible meanings of this present parable to them, Jesus complies with his disciples' request and enumerates its allegory point by point, revealing for the first time the identity of the Sower as the Son of man (Jesus himself).

The parables use the principle of "end stress" (in which the most important point of the parable is made at its conclusion), it helps make it clear that in contrast to the Sower's correlation between hearing and "growing," the emphasis of the Wheat and the Tares falls rather on its harvest imagery, and it is in fact a stark parable of the Last Judgment designed to reach a rural audience.

Spelled out for the benefit of the bemused disciples, the metaphor of the end of the world as a harvest was not an entirely novel one—earlier in the Gospel John the Baptist prophetically describes Jesus as one "whose fall is in his hand, and he will thoroughly purge his floor, and gather his wheat into the garner; but he will burn up the chaff with unquenchable fire." Jesus' message is unequivocal, and having described the horror and misery awaiting "the children of the wicked one," he returns to his earlier theme, urging, "Who hath ears to hear, let him hear," and offering his audience the chance to mend their ways before it is too late.

THE PARABLE OF THE MUSTARD SEED

MATTHEW 13:31–32

Another parable put he forth unto them, saying, The kingdom of heaven is like to a grain of mustard seed, which a man took, and sowed in his field:

Which indeed is the least of all seeds: but when it is grown, it is the greatest among herbs, and becometh a tree, so that the birds of the air come and lodge in the branches thereof.

MARK 4:30–32

And he said, Whereunto shall we liken the kingdom of God? or with what comparison shall we compare it?

It is like a grain of mustard seed, which, when it is sown in the earth, is less than all the seeds that be in the earth:

But when it is sown, it groweth up, and becometh greater than all herbs, and shooteth out great branches; so that the fowls of the air may lodge under the shadow of it.

LUKE 13:18–19

Then said he, Unto what is the kingdom of God like? and whereunto shall I resemble it?

It is like a grain of mustard seed, which a man took, and cast into his garden; and it grew, and waxed a great tree; and the fowls of the air lodged in the branches of it.

THE PARABLE OF THE LEAVEN

MATTHEW 13:33

Another parable spake he unto them; The kingdom of heaven is like unto leaven, which a woman took, and hid in three measures of meal, till the whole was leavened.

LUKE 13:20–21

And again he said, Whereunto shall I liken the kingdom of God?

It is like leaven, which a woman took and hid in three measures of meal, till the whole was leavened.

COMMENTARY

Paired together by Matthew and Luke, these two parables continue Jesus' exploration of the kingdom of heaven. In a ploy characteristic of the parable format, Jesus draws his images from the everyday and here applies them to a highly abstract concept—the kingdom of heaven. What could be more tangible than a tree, more readily understood than a loaf of bread, and yet, at the same time, more mysterious than the germination of a seed, the action of yeast in dough?

Again using images of organic growth, Jesus teaches that great things can emerge from small, inauspicious beginnings (a familiar concept to later audiences for whom the triumph of Jesus, a humble carpenter, was a given but which was by no means evident to Jesus' historical audience, who expected the glorious kingdom of heaven to be inaugurated by a mighty prince or warrior). As in the Parable of the Sower, it is the outcome of the growth that is significant; the disparity between the sizes of seed and tree heightens the achievement of the tiny mustard seed, while the successful leavening of the three measures of flour testifies to the thoroughness of the "growth."

In contrast to the apocalyptical sentiments of the Parable of the Wheat and Tares, the parables of the Mustard Seed and the Leaven are optimistic and life affirming. Indeed the disproportionate potential of the mustard seed and the apparently prosaic nature of the leaven are illustrative of the very nature of parables themselves. Often short, seemingly inconsequential sayings and stories, parables emerge from closer study as complex structures whose deceptive simplicity can support myriad meanings (some

Sir John Everett Millais, *The Leaven*
1864, wood engraving

A straightforward scene of domestic activity in harmony with the simplicity of the original parable.

conflicting) while carrying numerous allusions and considerable intertextuality. Proving the point, the pithy Parable of the Mustard Seed touches on the popular conception of Israel as a cedar tree and looks back to not one but two Old Testament books, recalling God's words in Ezekiel 17:22–23 and King Nebuchadnezzar's dream in Daniel 4:10–12:

. . . I saw, and behold a tree in the midst of the earth, and the height thereof was great. The tree grew, and was strong, and the height thereof reached unto

heaven, and the sight thereof to the end of all the earth: The leaves thereof were fair, and the fruit thereof much, and it was meat for all: the beasts of the field had shadow under it, and the fowls of the heaven dwelt in the boughs thereof, and all flesh was fed on it.

Luke records another reference to the mustard seed and its traditionally diminutive size later in his Gospel, 17:6: "And the Lord said, If ye had faith as a mustard seed, ye might say unto this sycamine tree, Be thou plucked up by the root, and be thou planted in the sea; and it should obey you."

THE PARABLE OF THE PEARL OF GREAT PRICE

MATTHEW 13:45–46

Again, the kingdom of heaven is like unto a merchant man, seeking goodly pearls;

Who, when he had found one pearl of great price, went and sold all that he had, and bought it.

COMMENTARY

Matthew's orderly arrangement of his Gospel material has been noted by commentators, and his penchant for numerical groupings of events—often in pairs or threes—is evident in these two parables. The parables of the Treasure in the Field and the Pearl of Great Price tell the stories of two men who each unexpectedly come across a valuable item, and who sell all their possessions to secure it. The status of the men—one a (presumably poor) hired farmhand, the other a (presumably rich) merchant—makes no difference to their responses. Both men recognize an opportunity, too good to be missed, and do not hesitate to risk everything to be part of it; this, Jesus teaches, is how we should respond to the kingdom of heaven. Moving on from earlier parables concerned with hearing, these stories are parables of action. If this is how wholeheartedly men react to the discovery of earthly treasure, how much more decisively, Jesus infers, should we act at the prospect of God's kingdom and its heavenly treasure.

DOMENICO FETTI, *THE PEARL OF GREAT PRICE*
c. 1618–19, oil on wood panel
The Nelson-Atkins Museum of Art, Kansas City, Missouri (Purchase: Nelson Trust)

A masterpiece of concision, the entire narrative of the Treasure in the Field is contained within a single sentence, relating not only an extraordinary sequence of events but also the joy experienced by the lucky ploughman. The image of exchanging one set of riches for another is a powerful one, appealing to mankind's deep-rooted respect for wealth, and later in Matthew's Gospel Jesus uses the same idea but more explicitly exposes the dichotomy between earthly wealth and heavenly riches: "If thou wilt be perfect, go and sell that thou hast, and give to the poor, and thou shalt have treasure in heaven."

THE PARABLE OF THE DRAGNET

MATTHEW 13:47–50

Again, the kingdom of heaven is like unto a net, that was cast into the sea, and gathered of every kind:

Which, when it was full, they drew to shore, and sat down, and gathered the good into vessels, but cast the bad away.

So shall it be at the end of the world: the angels shall come forth, and sever the wicked from among the just,

And shall cast them into the furnace of fire: there shall be wailing and gnashing of teeth.

COMMENTARY

Although grouped with the parables of the Treasure in the Field and the Pearl of Great Price, this parable is more akin to that of the Wheat and the Tares, sharing its somber vision of the Last Judgment. Jesus' choice of a fishing metaphor exploits another familiar aspect of first-century Palestinian life, echoing his call to fishermen Simon Peter and Andrew: "Follow me, and I will make you fishers of men."

In a paradox typical of many parables, the cool wet of the sea stands for its complete opposite, a "furnace of fire," but unlike with the Parable of the Wheat and the Tares, Jesus does not wait for his disciples to query his meaning and, unprompted, clearly outlines the fate awaiting the "bad fish" at the end of the world.

Jesus' vision of the end of the world is stark but, perhaps remembering the disciples' earlier incomprehension, he checks that his message has gone home: "Have ye understood all these things?" This time his followers are in no doubt: "They say unto him, Yea Lord."

BURLISON AND GRYLLS, *THE DRAGNET*
1875, stained glass
Photo: Copyright Sonia Halliday and Laura Lushington

A brightly colored, action-packed example of a nineteenth-century stained-glass church window. Unlike the medieval glass it sought to emulate, the parable's narrative has been compressed into a single scene.

MATTHEW 18:12–14

How think ye? if a man have an hundred sheep, and one of them be gone astray, doth he not leave the ninety and nine, and goeth into the mountains, and seeketh that which is gone astray?

And if so be that he find it, verily I say unto you, he rejoiceth more of that sheep, than of the ninety and nine which went not astray?

Even so it is not the will of your Father which is in heaven, that one of these little ones should perish.

LUKE 15:3–7

And he spake this parable unto them, saying,

What man of you, having an hundred sheep, if he lose one of them, doth not leave the ninety and nine in the wilderness, and go after that which is lost, until he find it?

And when he hath found it, he layeth it on his shoulders, rejoicing.

And when he cometh home, he calleth together his friends and neighbors, saying unto them, Rejoice with me; for I have found my sheep which was lost.

I say unto you, that likewise joy shall be in heaven over one sinner that repenteth, more than over ninety and nine just persons, which need no repentance.

COMMENTARY

The two versions of this parable are similar, but a brief comparison exemplifies how two Gospels can vary in approach and interpretation. In Matthew's account, the parable is Jesus' response to the disciples' question "Who is the greatest in the kingdom of heaven?" and forms part of his sermon on the role of children in God's kingdom. For Luke, however, the Lost Sheep is a riposte to the Pharisees' and scribes' criticism of Jesus' fellowship with sinners: "This man receiveth sinners, and eateth with them." Luke's version is the first of three parables on the theme of "lost and found," a sequence which culminates in the Parable of the Prodigal Son.

DOMENICO FETTI, *THE PARABLE OF THE LOST SHEEP*
before 1621, oil on poplar wood
Staatliche Kunstsammlungen Dresden

WILLIAM HOLMAN HUNT, *OUR ENGLISH COASTS (STRAYED SHEEP)*
1852, oil on canvas
© Tate Gallery, London

The sheep in this painting were only given a Christian connotation some years after the canvas was completed. Originally the "strayed sheep" were intended to illustrate the inadequacy of volunteer soldiers against a potential French invasion of England.

Both versions are framed as questions, parables designed to encourage Jesus' listeners (critics or converts) to think for themselves. As in the Parable of the Sower, Jesus is not interested in providing easy answers for his audience; the differing contexts of each version, however, help interpretation, and while Mark's emerges as an illustration of the need to defend the "little ones" as well as a visualization of Jesus' own mission as the "Good Shepherd," tending the "lost sheep of Israel," Luke's emphasis rests on the redemption of repentant sinners.

The two authors' narratives also differ in small but equally significant ways. Matthew states his case plainly, and although the finder of the stray sheep is expected to rejoice, the finding itself is uncertain: "And if so be that he find it . . ." In contrast, Luke replaces Matthew's "if" with a more optimistic "when"; his shepherd tenderly carries home the recovered stray and insists on sharing his happiness with friends and neighbors. Jesus likens the shepherd's joy to God's joy at welcoming repentant sinners into his kingdom and so discredits the Pharisees, whose holier-than-thou disparagement equates them with those who "need no repentance" (the sheep who did not go astray), and whose obedience gives God no cause for rejoicing.

THE PARABLE OF THE TREASURE IN THE FIELD

MATTHEW 13:44

Again, the kingdom of heaven is like unto treasure hid in a field, the which when a man hath found, he hideth, and for joy thereof goeth and selleth all that he hath, and buyeth that field.

JAMES TISSOT, *THE HIDDEN TREASURE*
1886–94, gouache on paperboard
The Brooklyn Museum 00.159.73, purchased by Public Subscription

Abandoning the modern-day settings of his Prodigal Son series, Tissot tried in his illustrations to The Life of Christ *to portray New Testament events with greater authenticity. The laborer who unearths the hidden treasure succumbs to a very human instinct and furtively glances over his shoulder to check whether his discovery has been witnessed by anyone else.*

MATTHEW 18:23–35

Therefore is the kingdom of heaven likened unto a certain king, which would take account of his servants.

And when he had begun to reckon, one was brought unto him, which owed him ten thousand talents.

But forasmuch as he had not to pay, his lord commanded him to be sold, and his wife, and children, and all that he had, and payment to be made.

The servant therefore fell down, and worshipped him, saying, Lord, have patience with me, and I will pay thee all.

Then the lord of that servant was moved with compassion, and loosed him, and forgave him the debt.

But the same servant went out, and found one of his fellowservants, which owed him an hundred pence: and he laid hands on him, and took him by the throat, saying, Pay me that thou owest.

And his fellowservant fell down at his feet, and besought him, saying, Have patience with me, and I will pay thee all.

And he would not: but went and cast him into prison, till he should pay the debt.

So when his fellowservants saw what was done, they were very sorry, and came and told unto their lord all that was done.

Then his lord, after that he had called him, said unto him, O thou wicked servant, I forgave thee all that debt, because thou desiredst me:

Shouldest not thou also have had compassion on thy fellowservant, even as I had pity on thee?

And his lord was wroth, and delivered him to the tormentors, till he should pay all that was due unto him.

So likewise shall my heavenly Father do also unto you, if ye from your hearts forgive not every one his brother their trespasses.

DOMENICO FETTI, *THE PARABLE OF THE UNMERCIFUL SERVANT*
pre-1621, oil on poplar wood
Staatliche Kunstsammlungen Dresden

In his uncompromising presentation of the parable, Fetti leaves the viewer in no doubt about the brutality of the unjust debtor.

This parable is part of Jesus' response to Peter's question "Lord, how oft shall my brother sin against me, and I forgive him?" Continuing the theme of sin and repentance, Jesus locates this story in more exotic territory than was employed in the pastoral parable of the Lost Sheep and uses an extended narrative to remind Peter of the necessity for forgiving as well as being forgiven as a prerequisite for entry into the kingdom.

The debt of the first servant is huge, its size reflecting the Oriental storyteller's love of exaggeration but on a practical level stressing the generosity of the king's clemency. The contrast between the two debts makes the first servant's behavior even more outrageous, and not content with simply asking for the hundred pence, he assaults his colleague before flinging him into prison. The second servant's response to the demand for money repeats exactly the words used earlier by his tormentor, a repetition underlining the aggressor's ruthlessness. Justice, however, is done and the king amplifies the violence and hard-heartedness shown to the first debtor, supplementing prison with torture.

Jesus' audience would have readily recognized the king as a representation of God, and this parable demonstrates how the generous, forgiving God might also be an exacting and vengeful deity. Jesus uses accounting as a metaphor for the Last Judgment, and it is significant that while the two debts are enumerated exactly, no mention is made of how they were run up. The detail is not essential for the story, but its absence reminds us that the ability to overlook is a useful one in forgiveness, and the parables' conclusion echoes the reciprocal forgiveness advised by the Lord's Prayer:

> For if ye forgive men their trespasses, your heavenly Father will also forgive you: But if ye forgive not men their trespasses, neither will your Father forgive your trespasses.

THE PARABLE OF THE LABORERS IN THE VINEYARD

MATTHEW 20:1–16

For the kingdom of heaven is like unto a man that is an householder, which went out early in the morning to hire laborers into his vineyard.

And when he had agreed with the laborers for a penny a day, he sent them into his vineyard.

And he went out about the third hour, and saw others standing idle in the marketplace,

And said unto them; Go ye also into the vineyard, and whatsoever is right I will give you.

MAERTEN DE VOS, *THE PARABLE OF THE LABOURERS IN THE VINEYARD*
sixteenth century
Nationalmuseum, Stockholm
Photo: Hans Thorwid, SKM, Stockholm

The laborers' dissent over their pay lies at the heart of this genial, Italianate painting. The foreman and his wages clerk are besieged by dissatisfied workers, whose argumentative gestures are echoed by their colleagues outside the central throng. The dispute looks set to continue, however—other workers have yet to arrive back in town and can be seen making their way down from the vineyard; in the meantime, it would seem that everyone in this crowded scene is talking about the issue.

And they went their way.

Again he went out about the sixth and ninth hour, and did likewise.

And about the eleventh hour he went out, and found others standing idle, and saith unto them, Why stand ye here all the day idle?

They say unto him, Because no man hath hired us. He saith unto them, Go ye also into the vineyard; and whatsoever is right, that shall ye receive.

So when even was come, the lord of the vineyard saith unto his steward, Call the laborers, and give them their hire, beginning from the last unto the first.

And when they came that were hired about the eleventh hour, they received every man a penny.

But when the first came, they supposed that they should have received more; and they likewise received every man a penny.

And when they had received it, they murmured against the goodman of the house,

Saying, These last have wrought but one hour, and thou hast made them equal unto us, which have borne the burden and heat of the day.

But he answered one of them, and said, Friend, I do thee no wrong: didst not thou agree with me for a penny?

Take that thine is, and go thy way: I will give unto this last, even as unto thee.

Is it not lawful for me to do what I will with mine own? Is thine eye evil, because I am good?

So the last shall be first, and the first last: for many be called, but few chosen.

COMMENTARY

Picking up on an Old Testament image of Israel as God's vineyard, Jesus here casts God as a householder and those who strive to do his will as laborers. Earlier in the same Gospel he uses the theme of harvest to galvanize his followers, telling them, "The harvest truly is plenteous but the laborers are few." Here the connotation is rather different and it is the workers rather than the grapes they pick who are God's true harvest.

Although the sequence of hiring could imply an understaffed workforce, the main point of the parable is the nature of God's justice. The householder's generous—but evenhanded—behavior and the unjustified expectations of the first workers teaches that God's largesse cannot be bought or even earned but is bestowed entirely at his own discretion.

Jesus aimed this bittersweet parable at his fiercest critics, the Pharisees, playing the Pharisees at their own game. Jesus' narrative ensures that the complaints of the Pharisees' metaphoric counterparts—the laborers who work diligently all day—are confounded by the householder's scrupulous compliance with his original agreement. The laborers hired subsequently, who passively waited for work, are less evidently worthy than their industrious colleagues and represent sinners. The successive hours of the day and times of hiring are sometimes interpreted as an allegory of the different ages at which people receive God's call, but have also been read as an allegory of the development of the Church.

The authenticity of the final line has also been queried by some commentators, and does seem contrived and inaccurate, the parable demonstrating not that the first shall come last and vice versa but that everyone gets what they deserve (in the story all the workers receive the same wage). The concluding line reiterates the inverse order of wage paying, a literary device to ensure that the first laborers' expectations (and those of the audience) are raised, and then dashed as they witness the "unfair" payment, so that they can then raise their objections with the landowner, who is still on hand to respond to them.

MATTHEW 21:28–32

But what think ye? A certain man had two sons; and he came to the first, and said, Son, go work today in my vineyard.

He answered and said, I will not: but afterward he repented, and went.

And he came to the second, and said likewise. And he answered and said, I go, sir: and went not.

Whether of them twain did the will of his father? They say unto him, The first. Jesus saith unto them, Verily I say unto you, That the publicans and the harlots go into the kingdom of God before you.

For John came unto you in the way of righteousness, and ye believed him not: but the publicans and the harlots believed him: and ye, when ye had seen it, repented not afterward, that ye might believe him.

COMMENTARY

Refusing to recognize Jesus' true status as the Messiah, the religious establishment constantly questioned his authority to teach and heal the people. This parable results from just such an encounter between Jesus and the chief priests and elders of the temple. Jesus deflects their hostility by asking them their position on John the Baptist; sensing a trap, they decline to answer, and Jesus likewise refuses to justify himself, telling them the story of the two sons instead.

Like the previous parable, it demonstrates the supremacy of repentant sinners in the kingdom of heaven. Both sons are willful—typically human in this respect—but it is the first son's change of heart which sets him apart from his recalcitrant brother and enables him to obey his father. The second son simply pays lip service to his father's request and continues to disobey him.

The opening demand of the parable invites listeners to involve themselves in the moral dilemma, and it is clear Jesus wants his audience to make up their own minds. The scribes and elders respond correctly, but this time they have been snared; the answer tells against them, for Jesus goes on to relate the parable to their treatment of John the Baptist, their failure to give him credence even after prostitutes and tax collectors have acknowledged his righteousness. The inflexibility of the elders is contrasted against the sinners' willingness to repent—a situation no less relevant to Jesus' own mission—and the parable leaves no doubt as to which trait finds greatest favor in God's kingdom.

MATTHEW 21:33–44

Hear another parable: There was a certain householder, which planted a vineyard, and hedged it round about, and digged a winepress in it, and built a tower, and let it out to husbandmen, and went into a far country:

And when the time of the fruit drew near, he sent his servants to the husbandmen, that they might receive the fruits of it.

And the husbandmen took his servants, and beat one, and killed another, and stoned another.

Again, he sent other servants more than the first: and they did unto them likewise.

But last of all he sent unto them his son, saying, They will reverence my son.

But when the husbandmen saw the son, they said among themselves, This is the heir, come, let us kill him, and let us seize on his inheritance.

And they caught him, and cast him out of the vineyard, and slew him.

When the lord therefore of the vineyard cometh, what will he do unto those husbandmen?

They say unto him, He will miserably destroy those wicked men, and will let out his vineyard unto other husbandmen, which shall render him the fruits in their seasons.

Jesus saith unto them, Did ye never read in the scriptures, The stone which the builders rejected, the same is become the head of the corner: this is the Lord's doing, and it is marvellous in our eyes?

Therefore say I unto you, The kingdom of God shall be taken from you, and given to a nation bringing forth the fruits thereof.

And whosoever shall fall on this stone shall be broken: but on whomsoever it shall fall, it will grind him to powder.

MARK 12:1–11

And he began to speak unto them by parables. A certain man planted a vineyard, and set an hedge about it, and digged a place for the winefat, and built a tower, and let it out to husbandmen, and went into a far country.

SIR JOHN EVERETT MILLAIS, *THE WICKED HUSBANDMEN*
1864, wood engraving

The son of the master of the vineyard lies strangled at the gates of his father's property, his body half-hidden by tangled vegetation, a twisted vine around his neck the instrument of his death.

And at the season he sent to the husbandmen a servant, that he might receive from the husbandmen of the fruit of the vineyard.

And they caught him, and beat him, and sent him away empty.

And again he sent unto them another servant; and at him they cast stones, and wounded him in the head, and sent him away shamefully handled.

And again he sent another; and him they killed and many others; beating some, and killing some.

Having yet therefore one son, his wellbeloved, he sent him also last unto them, saying, They will reverence my son.

But those husbandmen said among themselves, This is the heir; come, let us kill him, and the inheritance shall be ours.

And they took him, and killed him, and cast him out of the vineyard.

What shall therefore the lord of the vineyard do? he will come and destroy the husbandmen, and will give the vineyard unto others.

And have ye not read this scripture; The stone which the builders rejected is become the head of the corner:

This was the Lord's doing, and it is marvellous in our eyes?

LUKE 20:9–19

Then began he to speak to the people this parable; A certain man planted a vineyard, and let it forth to husbandmen, and went into a far country for a long time.

And at the season he sent a servant to the husbandmen, that they should give him of the fruit of the vineyard: but the husbandmen beat him, and sent him away empty.

And again he sent another servant: and they beat him also, and entreated him shamefully, and sent him away empty.

And again he sent a third: and they wounded him also, and cast him out.

Then said the lord of the vineyard, What shall I do? I will send my beloved son: it may be they will reverence him when they see him.

But when the husbandmen saw him, they reasoned among themselves, saying, This is the heir: come, let us kill him, that the inheritance may be ours.

So they cast him out of the vineyard, and killed him. What therefore shall the lord of the vineyard do unto them?

He shall come and destroy these husbandmen, and shall give the vineyard to others. And when they heard it, they said, God forbid.

And he beheld them, and said, What is then that is written, The stone which the builders rejected, the same is become the head of the corner?

Whosoever shall fall upon that stone shall be broken; but on whomsoever it shall fall, it will grind him to powder.

And the chief priests and the scribes the same hour sought to lay hands on him; and they feared the people: for they perceived that he had spoken this parable against them.

COMMENTARY

Recounted by all three Synoptic authors, this is another parable in which Jesus turns the criticism of the chief priests and scribes back on themselves. Because they were an educated audience, well-versed in Scripture, the paraphrasing and quotation of Isaiah (the description of the planting of the vineyard) and Psalm 118 (the stone rejected by the builders) would have alerted them to the subtext of the parable—a shaming indictment of their failure as caretakers of God's kingdom. The servants they mistreat so callously represent the prophets of the Old Testament, while the landlord's well-beloved son (described in Luke as his only son) is of course Jesus. Drawing on ancient prophecy, the parable itself foretells Jesus' own death—the tenants' murder of the heir beyond the vineyard walls is a chilling rehearsal of the betrayal that would befall Jesus and his execution outside the city. The husbandmen's plan backfires, however, and precipitates the confiscation of the coveted vineyard; Matthew's version of the parable reiterates this outcome in a sequence of explanatory statements, Jesus first pressing his audience to predict the husbandmen's punishment, then quoting the prediction of Psalm 118, and finally explicitly relating the parable's conclusion to the temple elders.

Jesus' audience does indeed grasp the correct meaning of the parable but refuses to learn from its message, as Luke notes: "And the chief priests and the scribes the same hour sought to lay hands on him; and they feared the people: for they perceived that he had spoken this parable against them." Stung into action, the temple hierarchy renew their plotting against Jesus, inexorably fulfilling the prophecy of both psalm and parable.

THE PARABLE OF THE WEDDING FEAST

MATTHEW 22:2–14

The kingdom of heaven is like unto a certain king, which made a marriage for his son,

And sent forth his servants to call them that were bidden the wedding: and they would not come.

Again, he sent forth other servants, saying, Tell them which are bidden, Behold, I have prepared my dinner: my oxen and my fatlings are killed, and all things are ready: come unto the marriage.

BERNARDO STROZZI, *THE PARABLE OF THE WEDDING GUEST*
seventeenth century
Museo dell'Accademia ligustica di belle arti, Genova

Bound hand and foot with rope and guarded by three soldiers, the unkempt wedding guest prepares to be punished. The ovoid shape and dramatic low viewpoint of the painting emphasizes the well-like depth of the "outer darkness" into which he is about to be plunged.

But they made light of it, and went their ways, one to his farm, another to his merchandise:

And the remnant took his servants, and entreated them spitefully, and slew them.

But when the king heard thereof, he was wroth: and he sent forth his armies, and destroyed those murderers, and burned up their city.

Then saith he to his servants, The wedding is ready, but they which were bidden were not worthy.

Go ye therefore into the highways, and as many as ye shall find, bid to the marriage.

So those servants went out into the highways, and gathered together all as many as they found, both bad and good: and the wedding was furnished with guests.

And when the king came in to see the guests, he saw there a man which had not on a wedding garment:

And he saith unto him, Friend, how camest thou in hither not having a wedding garment?

And he was speechless.

Then said the king to the servants, Bind him hand and foot, and take him away, and cast him into outer darkness; there shall be weeping and gnashing of teeth.

For many are called, but few are chosen.

THE PARABLE OF THE GREAT SUPPER

LUKE 14:15–24

And when one of them that sat at meat with him heard these things, he said unto him, Blessed is he that shall eat bread in the kingdom of God.

Then said he unto them, A certain man made a great supper, and bade many:

And sent his servant at supper time to say to them that were bidden, Come; for all things are now ready.

And they all with one consent began to make excuse. The first said unto him, I have bought a piece of ground, and I must needs go and see it: I pray thee have me excused.

And another said, I have bought five yoke of oxen, and I go to prove them: I pray thee have me excused.

And another said, I have married a wife, and therefore I cannot come.

So that servant came, and shewed his lord these things. Then the master of the house being angry said to his servant, Go out quickly into the streets and lanes of the city, and bring in hither the poor, and the maimed, and the halt, and the blind.

And the servant said, Lord, it is done as thou hast commanded, and yet there is room.

And the lord said unto the servant, Go out into the highways and hedges, and compel them to come in, that my house may be filled.

For I say unto you, That none of those men which were bidden shall taste of my supper.

COMMENTARY

Jesus' opponents were implacable in their resistance to him. As in the Parable of the Wicked Tenants, these parables narrate the rejection of God's kingdom by some but also show how that denial facilitates entry for others. Likening the kingdom to a celebratory meal, the Gospelists demonstrate God's hospitality and generosity, by the same token underlining the churlishness of those who renege on their invitations with flimsy excuses.

While they are variants of the same story, Luke's account is the more optimistic of the two and avoids the violence of Matthew's version. The spurned host sends his servants out again to replenish the guest list, specifying exactly who he wants to invite, "the poor, and the maimed, and the halt, and the blind," categories that correspond exactly to those types of people ministered to by Jesus himself. This instruction is followed by another, less exacting, one, recalling the mission of Jesus' "servants," the disciples, and no doubt reflecting Luke's concern to demonstrate the universal accessibility of God's kingdom. The host's invitation to the outcasts of society puts into action Jesus' advice to a Pharisee who wanted to invite him for a meal: "But when thou makest a feast, call the poor, the maimed, the lame, the blind: And thou shalt be blessed; for they cannot recompense thee: for thou shalt be recompensed at the resurrection of the just."

The Gospels abound with references to meals taken or presided over by Jesus—the feeding of the five thousand, his table fellowship with sinners such as Zacchaeus—and Luke's parable (itself about a feast) is framed with precise references to food and eating. The final line anticipates the Last Supper and its symbolism of bread as the body of Christ; the denial of "my supper" to the originally invited guest seems mild (compared to the destruction meted out in Matthew's version), but its symbolic import is profound.

Matthew's version, punctuated with violence and heavy with symbolism, is complicated by the additional parable embedded in its text. Matthew's story of the Wedding Guest contradicts Luke's humane vision; describing a vengeful God and a forbidding heavenly kingdom, Matthew sounds a warning note: "Many are called, but few are chosen." Matthew's narrative is full of portent: The host is a king, preparing a lavish wedding feast for his son (the image of Jesus as bridegroom recurs in the Parable of the Wise and Foolish Virgins), the reprisal against the first invited guests is swift and conclusive, and the annihilation of their city has been interpreted as a reference to the sack of Jerusalem. Matthew is less concerned with the characteristics of the subsequent guests, content simply to record them as "good" and "bad" before drawing our attention to the transgression and violent end of the latter.

THE PARABLE OF THE THIEF IN THE NIGHT

MATTHEW 24:42–44

Watch therefore: for ye know not what hour your Lord doth come.

But know this, that if the goodman of the house had known in what watch the thief would come, he would have watched, and would not have suffered his house to be broken up.

Therefore be ye also ready: for in such an hour as ye think not the Son of man cometh.

LUKE 12:39–40

And this know, that it the goodman of the house had known what hour the thief would come, he would have watched, and not have suffered his house to be broken through.

Be ye therefore ready also: for the Son of man cometh at an hour when ye think not.

THE PARABLE OF THE FAITHFUL AND UNFAITHFUL SERVANT

MATTHEW 24:45–51

Who then is a faithful and wise servant, whom his lord hath made ruler over his household, to give them meat in due season?

Blessed is that servant, whom his lord when he cometh shall find so doing.

Verily I say unto you, That he shall make him ruler over all his goods.

But it that evil servant shall say in his heart, My lord delayeth his coming;

And shall begin to smite his fellow-servants, and to eat and drink with the drunken;

The lord of that servant shall come in a day when he looketh not for him, and in an hour that he is not aware of,

And shall cut him asunder, and appoint him his portion with the hypocrites: there shall be weeping and gnashing of teeth.

And the Lord said, Who then is that faithful and wise steward, whom his lord shall make ruler over his household, to give them their portion of meat in due season?

Blessed is that servant, whom his lord when he cometh shall find so doing.

Of a truth I say unto you, that he will make him ruler over all that he hath.

But and if that servant say in his heart, My lord delayeth his coming; and shall begin to beat the menservants and maidens, and to eat and drink, and to be drunken;

The lord of that servant will come in a day when he looketh not for him, and at an hour when he is not aware, and will cut him in sunder, and will appoint him his portion with the unbelievers.

And that servant, which knew his lord's will, and prepared not himself, neither did according to his will, shall be beaten with many stripes.

But he that knew not, and did commit things worthy of stripes, shall be beaten with few stripes. For unto whomsoever much is given, of him shall be much required: and to whom men have committed much, of him they will ask the more.

THE PARABLE OF THE PORTER

MARK 13:34-37

For the Son of man is as a man taking a far journey, who left his house, and gave authority to his servants, and to every man his work, and commanded the porter to watch.

Watch ye therefore: for ye know not when the master of the house cometh, at even, or at midnight, or at the cock-crowing, or in the morning:

Lest coming suddenly he find you sleeping.

And what I say unto you I say unto all, Watch.

THE PARABLE OF THE WATCHMAN

LUKE 12:36-38

And ye yourselves be like unto men that wait for their lord, when he will return from the wedding; that when he cometh and knocketh, they may open unto him immediately.

Blessed are those servants, whom the lord when he cometh shall find watching: verily I say unto you, that he shall gird himself, and make them to sit down to meat, and will come forth and serve them.

And if he shall come in the second watch, or come in the third watch, and find them so, blessed are those servants.

COMMENTARY

Although for some Jesus heralded the arrival of God's kingdom, this group of parables suggest how Jesus saw the kingdom of heaven as an ongoing event, its final establishment taking place in the future and coinciding with his Second Coming. The parables are primarily a response to some disciples who wanted to know (as recorded by Matthew) "when shall these things be? and what shall be the sign of thy coming, and of the end of the world?"

The parables' theme of waiting and watching indicates that some delay was to be expected before the kingdom's complete establishment, and Jesus' followers are explicitly instructed to wait and be prepared for this eventuality: "Watch ye therefore," "Be ye also ready." The absent householder and the elapse of time specified in Mark's Parable of the Porter and Luke's version of the Thief in the Night would have been particularly poignant for the early Church, eagerly awaiting what they believed to be the imminent arrival of the kingdom, but coming to terms with its continued nonappearance. These parables were no less urgent for Jesus' actual audience. As crisis deepened around him and his Crucifixion drew near, Jesus urged his disciples to be alert, to be ready to help him when he called. Just before his betrayal by Judas, Jesus, wanting to pray alone, asked his disciples to "Tarry ye here, and watch with me," but this and his earlier pleas go unheeded when Peter and his companions fall asleep while their master prays.

Complementing the theme of delay, the Parable of the Thief in the Night counsels preparedness in the face of the unexpected arrival of the kingdom. The image of a burglar unobtrusively breaking into a house without warning was also used by Saint Paul in his first letter to the Thessalonians: "For yourselves know perfectly well that the day of the Lord cometh as a thief in the night." The unexpected return of the householder in the Parable of the Faithful and Unfaithful Servants also urges watchfulness but at the same time stresses the need for correct conduct in his absence. The obedient servant is generously rewarded, but the other, who deceives and so betrays his master, is swiftly punished. His behavior recalls that of the Wicked Tenants, and the parable can also be read as another attack on the Pharisees and their treachery.

MATTHEW 25:1–13

Then shall the kingdom of heaven be likened unto ten virgins, which took their lamps, and went forth to meet the bridegroom.

And five of them were wise, and five were foolish.

They that were foolish took their lamps, and took no oil with them:

But the wise took oil in their vessels with their lamps.

While the bridegroom tarried, they all slumbered and slept.

And at midnight there was a cry made, Behold, the bridegroom cometh; go ye out to meet him.

Then all those virgins arose, and trimmed their lamps.

And the foolish said unto the wise, Give us of your oil; for our lamps are gone out.

But the wise answered, saying, Not so; lest there be not enough for us and you; but go ye rather to them that sell, and buy for yourselves.

And while they went to buy, the bridegroom came; and they that were ready went in with him to the marriage: and the door was shut.

Afterward came also the other virgins, saying, Lord, Lord, open to us.

But he answered and said, Verily I say unto you, I know you not.

Watch therefore, for ye know neither the day nor the hour wherein the Son of man cometh.

COMMENTARY

Although Jesus often talked about the arrival of the kingdom, the timing of this event remained unspecified and this parable suggests that the kingdom might be delayed longer than expected. Faced with a lengthy wait before the bridegroom's arrival, all ten bridesmaids—wise and foolish alike—quite understandably fall asleep. The foolishness of five lies not, however, in their slumber but rather in their failure to anticipate an extended vigil and to bring any oil for this eventuality. The Wise Virgins' refusal to lend them oil seems uncharitable but is a further display of their prudence—they have brought along just enough oil for the evening. By the time the Foolish Bridesmaids have replenished their lamps, they are late for the wedding feast and are refused admission. The bridesmaids are required to wait for the groom, but the groom will not wait for his attendants, and even denies knowledge of them.

The outcome, though harsh, is not entirely unexpected. Because the bridesmaids have been described as "wise" or "foolish" from the start, the audience expects the wise virgins to triumph, the foolish to fail. The parable doesn't present a moral dilemma, it

JACOPO TINTORETTO, *THE WISE AND FOOLISH VIRGINS*
c. 1548, oil
Photo: National Trust Photographic Library/Angelo Hornak

Having belatedly bought oil for their lamps, the Foolish Virgins return to the wedding only to find the door has already been locked. The Bridegroom and Wise Virgins look down at them from the upper level of the balcony, immune to their pleading.

simply juxtaposes wise and foolish, ready and not ready, to demonstrate preparedness as a prerequisite for entry into the kingdom of heaven. To Jesus' original audience, the parable would have had the same intention as the other parables of this group: to arouse listeners to realize the gravity of the current situation and to be ready for the crisis bought about by Jesus' mission. To the developing Christian Church, they were interpreted as parables of the *parousia* (the Greek term for Christ's Second Coming), warnings to the community not to lose hope of the kingdom despite the ever-lengthening delay in its arrival.

THE PARABLE OF THE TALENTS

MATTHEW 25:14–30

For the kingdom of heaven is as a man traveling into a far country, who called his own servants, and delivered unto them his goods.

And unto one he gave five talents, to another two, and to another one; to every man according to his several ability; and straightway took his journey.

Then he that had received the five talents went and traded with the same, and made them other five talents.

And likewise he that had received two, he also gained other two.

But he that had received one went and digged in the earth, and hid his lord's money.

After a long time the lord of those servants cometh, and reckoneth with them.

And so he that had received five talents came and brought other five talents, saying, Lord, thou deliveredst unto me five talents: behold, I have gained beside them five talents more.

His lord said unto him, Well done, thou good and faithful servant: thou hast been faithful over a few things, I will make thee ruler over many things: enter thou into the joy of thy lord.

He also that had received two talents came and said, Lord, thou deliveredst unto me two talents: behold, I have gained two other talents beside them.

His lord said unto him, Well done, good and faithful servant: thou hast been faithful over a few things, I will make thee ruler over many things: enter thou into the joy of thy lord.

Then he which had received the one talent came and said, Lord, I knew thee that thou art an hard man, reaping where thou hast not sown, and gathering where thou hast not strawed:

And I was afraid, and went and hid thy talent in the earth: lo, there thou hast that is thine.

His lord answered and said unto him, Thou wicked and slothful servant: thou knewest that I reap where I sowed not, and gather where I have not strawed:

Thou oughtest therefore to have put my money to the exchangers, and then at my coming I should have received mine own with usury.

Take therefore the talent from him, and give it unto him which hath ten talents.

For unto every one that hath shall be given, and he shall have abundance: but from him that hath not shall be taken away even that which he hath.

And cast ye the unprofitable servant into outer darkness: there shall be weeping and gnashing of teeth.

THE PARABLE OF THE POUNDS

LUKE 19:11–27

And as they heard these things, he added and spake a parable, because he was nigh to Jerusalem, and because they thought that the kingdom of God should immediately appear.

He said therefore, A certain nobleman went into a far country to receive for himself a kingdom, and to return.

And he called his ten servants, and delivered them ten pounds, and said unto them, Occupy till I come.

But his citizens hated him, and sent a message after him, saying, We will not have this man reign over us.

And it came to pass, that when he was returned, having received the kingdom, then he commanded these servants to be called unto him, to whom he had given the money, that he might know how much every man had gained by trading.

Then came the first, saying, Lord, thy pound hath gained ten pounds.

And he said unto him, Well, thou good servant: because thou hast been faithful in a very little, have thou authority over ten cities.

And the second came, saying, Lord, thy pound hath gained five pounds.

And he said likewise to him, Be thou also over five cities.

And another came, saying, Lord, behold, here is thy pound, which I have kept laid up in a napkin:

For I feared thee, because thou art an austere man: thou takest up that thou layedst not down, and reapest that thou didst not sow.

And he saith unto him, Out of thine own mouth will I judge thee, thou wicked servant. Thou knewest that I was an austere man, taking up that I laid not down, and reaping that I did not sow.

Wherefore then gavest not thou my money into the bank, that at my coming I might have required mine own with usury.

And he said unto them that stood by, Take from him the pound, and give it to him that hath ten pounds,

(And they said unto him, Lord, he hath ten pounds.)

For I say unto you, That unto every one which hath shall be given; and from him that hath not, even that he hath shall be taken away from him.

But those mine enemies, which would not that I should reign over them, bring hither, and slay them before me.

COMMENTARY

This is another *parousia* parable, in which Jesus returns to the image of servants being left alone while their master is away. As in the Parable of the Faithful and Unfaithful Servants, this parable teaches the need for loyalty and responsibility during the wait for God's kingdom. Entrusted, commensurate with their individual abilities, with their master's wealth, the majority of servants invest the money profitably, and are rewarded when the master returns to take account of his affairs. The least able servant is paralyzed by fear of his allegedly unjust master and, refusing to take the necessary risk, voids the money's potential, thus betraying his master. Unlike the servant who uncovers hidden wealth in the Parable of the Treasure in the Field, he buries his talent. Although under rabbinic law the burying of a surety was deemed the best way of safeguarding it, and in case of theft legally freed its guardian of liability, the parable implies that, at the Day of Judgment, God will expect a return on his investments and welcomes risk takers.

Luke's version of the parable contains a further betrayal in his additional story of the nobleman receiving a kingdom. This embellishment was based on an historical event: in the fourth century B.C., when Archelaus was made governor of Judea, a delegation of Jews preceded him to Rome to resist the appointment. When Archelaus returned to Judea as governor, he exacted a bloody revenge for his subjects' disloyalty—a reprisal perhaps still in the living memory of Jesus' original audience. In Luke the placing of the parable is particularly significant; being narrated on Jesus' final journey to Jerusalem, when his own betrayal was imminent, it precedes the Parable of the Wicked Tenants, another story pillorying the Pharisees for their rejection of the Messiah.

THE PARABLE OF THE SEED GROWING SECRETLY

MARK 4:26–29

And he said, So is the kingdom of God, as if a man should cast seed into the ground;

And should sleep, and rise night and day, and the seed should spring and grow up, he knoweth not how.

For the earth bringeth forth fruit of herself; first the blade, then the ear, and after that the full corn in the ear.

But when the fruit is brought forth, immediately he putteth in the sickle, because the harvest is come.

COMMENTARY

Unique to his gospel, Mark positioned this parable between his accounts of the Sower and the Mustard Seed. Jesus' description of seed growing successfully to maturity without human intervention—or even understanding—evokes the mystery and power of his Father's kingdom. The parable shows that, in the same way that man has no authority over nature, he has no influence over God's domain, but the final harvest image also illustrates man's ability to recognize when his participation in God's work is required.

THE PARABLE OF THE TWO DEBTORS

LUKE 7:41–43

There was a certain creditor which had two debtors: the one owed five hundred pence, and the other fifty.

And when they had nothing to pay, he frankly forgave them both. Tell me therefore, which of them will love him most?

Simon answered and said, I suppose that he, to whom he forgave most. And he said unto him, Thou hast rightly judged.

COMMENTARY

Jesus addressed this parable to a Pharisee who had invited him to his house for a meal. There Jesus allowed his feet to be anointed by a townswoman, much to his host's silently expressed indignation: "This man, if he were a prophet, would have known who and what manner of woman this is that toucheth him: for she is a sinner."

Jesus' response—a parable posed as a question—disarms the Pharisee's unspoken criticism. Common throughout Jesus' parables, financial imagery is used here, as in the Parable of the Unforgiving Debtor, to expose the true nature of forgiveness. Although the dramatis personae remain anonymous, Luke enumerates the two debts exactly, showing the audience how much is at stake for the two debtors, while the cancellation of the debts demonstrates the reciprocal relationship between forgiveness and love. Once again, the Pharisees' correct answer works against him. Jesus contrasts the host's indifferent hospitality with the care lavished on him by the woman: "I entered into thine house, thou gavest me no water for my feet: but she hath washed my feet with tears," and he goes on to conclude: "Her sins, which are many, are forgiven: for she loved much: but to whom little is forgiven, the same loveth little."

THE PARABLE OF THE GOOD SAMARITAN

LUKE 10:25–37

And, behold, a certain lawyer stood up, and tempted him, saying, Master, what shall I do to inherit eternal life?

He said unto him, What is written in the law? how readest thou?

And he answering said, Thou shalt love the Lord thy God with all thy heart, and with all thy soul, and with all thy strength, and with all thy mind; and thy neighbor as to thyself.

And he said unto him, Thou hast answered right: this do, and thou shalt live.

But he, willing to justify himself, said unto Jesus, And who is my neighbor?

And Jesus answering said, A certain man went down from Jerusalem to Jericho, and fell among thieves, which stripped him of his raiment, and wounded him, and departed, leaving him half dead.

And by chance there came down a certain priest that way: and when he saw him, he passed by on the other side.

And likewise a Levite, when he was at the place, came and looked on him, and passed by on the other side.

But a certain Samaritan, as he journeyed, came where he was: and when he saw him, he had compassion on him,

And went to him, and bound up his wounds, pouring in oil and wine, and set him on his own beast, and brought him to an inn, and took care of him.

JACOPO BASSANO, *THE GOOD SAMARITAN*
sixteenth century, oil on canvas
The National Gallery, London, reproduced by courtesy of the Trustees

Bassano unflinchingly records the corpse-like pallor of the traveler, the seriousness of whose injuries underlines the inhumanity of the priest and Levite who hurry past in the background.

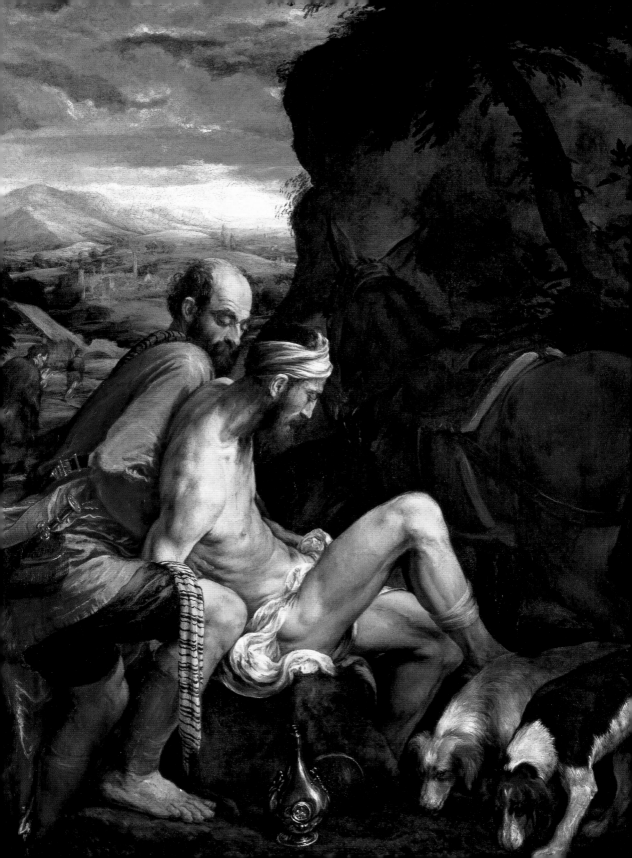

And on the morrow when he departed, he took out two pence, and gave them to the host, and said unto him, Take care of him; and whatsoever thou spendest more, when I come again, I will repay thee.

Which now of these three, thinkest thou, was neighbor unto him that fell among the thieves?

And he said, He that shewed mercy on him. Then said Jesus unto him, Go, and do thou likewise.

COMMENTARY

One of the best-loved and most well-known of all Jesus' parables, this story has taught generations the concept of good neighborliness. No doubt the lawyer who questioned Jesus about eternal life expected to be provided with a neat formula of behavior. Jesus, however, re-presents the question at the end of the story, forcing the lawyer to answer it for himself.

The story contrasts a humane, compassionate approach to life with one bounded by rigid legalistic constraints, as practiced by the Pharisees and typified here by the callous reaction of the priest and the Levite (temple workers both) and their refusal to help a stricken fellowman. The example of the Samaritan as good neighbor would have been startling to Jesus' audience, who would have expected him to contrast the religious types with an ordinary layperson. There was a long history of conflict between Israelites and Samaritans—each side hated the other—but the parable resonates with another "good deed" by Samaritans, recorded in 2 Chronicles 28, in which they tend battle-wounded Israelites and escort them back to Jerusalem on their beasts. Jesus used the Samaritan to shock his Jewish audience out of their complacency, as the story shows a reviled outsider complying with the spirit of Jewish law better than religious people. The unflattering presentation of Pharisee and Levite would have been equally shocking—a harsh critique of the upper echelons of Jewish religion.

The Samaritan's compassion sets him apart. He unquestioningly helps the victim, in contrast to the temple workers who evaluate the situation before deciding not to help and the insistent questioning of the lawyer himself. Despite the parable's shock value, the tone is restrained, with the Samaritan's actions exactly fitting the needs of the situation: He tends his patient's wounds with oil (an emollient) and wine (a disinfectant), transports him to an inn, makes a fair and sensible arrangement with the landlord there, and continues on with his business.

WILLIAM HOLMAN HUNT, *THE IMPORTUNATE NEIGHBOUR*
1895, oil on canvas on wood
National Gallery of Victoria, Melbourne, Australia, Felton Bequest, 1905

Even the dogs, who drink from a water bowl in the starlit courtyard, are shown more hospitality than the man who tries to borrow some bread from his neighbor.

THE PARABLE OF THE FRIEND AT MIDNIGHT

LUKE 11:5–10

And he said unto them, Which of you shall have a friend, and shall go unto him at midnight, and say unto him, Friend, lend me three loaves;

For a friend of mine in his journey is come to me, and I have nothing to set before him?

And he from within shall answer and say, Trouble me not: the door is now shut, and my children are with me in bed; I cannot rise and give thee.

I say unto you, Though he will not rise and give him, because he is a friend, yet because of his importunity he will rise and give him as many as he needeth.

And I say unto you, Ask, and it shall be given you; seek, and ye shall find; knock, and it shall be opened unto you.

For every one that asketh receiveth; and he that seeketh findeth; and to him that knocketh it shall be opened.

COMMENTARY

Like the Parable of the Good Samaritan, this parable concerns an individual in need of help. Eschewing the drama of the notoriously bandit-infested Jerusalem-Jericho road, Jesus now describes a purely domestic crisis. The parable was designed to demonstrate the power of prayer, and Luke aptly locates it immediately after Jesus teaches his disciples the Lord's Prayer. Both prayer and parable answer the disciples' initial request, "Teach us to pray." Using a scenario from everyday life, the parable indicates how favorably God will respond to prayer and perseverance of faith, if this is how an ordinary man succumbs to a friend pestering him for a favor at an inconvenient time. Reminiscent of the parables of the Thief in the Night and the Watchman, the motif of an unexpected arrival is here duplicated—the traveler surprises his unprepared host, who in turn importunes his friend for the provisions that will enable him to provide hospitality. The parable could thus also suggest that if this is the effort a man will make to procure bread for a friend, how much more should we be prepared to pray to God, and how much greater will his reward for such faith be.

THE PARABLE OF THE RICH FOOL

LUKE 12:16–21

And he spake a parable unto them, saying, The ground of a certain rich man brought forth plentifully:

And he thought within himself, saying, What shall I do, because I have no room where to bestow my fruits?

And he said, This will I do: I will pull down my barns, and build greater; and there will I bestow all my fruits and my goods.

And I will say to my soul, Soul, thou hast much goods laid up for many years; take thine ease, eat, drink, and be merry.

But God said unto him, Thou fool, this night thy soul shall be required of thee: then whose shall those things be, which thou hast not provided?

So is he that layeth up treasure for himself, and is not rich toward God.

COMMENTARY

Teaching a large crowd, Jesus is asked by one of the audience to intervene in an inheritance dispute between two brothers. Jesus declines to get embroiled but uses the request as a springboard for a warning, "Take heed, and beware covetousness—for a man's life consisteth not in the abundance of the things which he possesseth." The parable reinforces this message, in that the worldly goods hoarded by the rich man are shown to be an irrelevance in God's kingdom. Despite his wealth, the man has no control over his destiny; his self-satisfied soliloquy to his soul becomes, whether he wills it or not, a dialogue with God, in which his unpreparedness for the kingdom is exposed. The rich man is indeed a fool; his priority should have been developing a profitable relationship with God, whose own concerns lie with spiritual, not material, commodities.

THE PARABLE OF THE BARREN FIG TREE

LUKE 13:6–9

He spake also this parable; A certain man had a fig tree planted in his vineyard; and he came and sought fruit thereon, and found none.

Then said he unto the dresser of his vineyard, Behold these three years I come seeking fruit on this fig tree, and find none, cut it down; why cumbereth it the ground?

And he answering said unto him, Lord let it alone this year also, till I shall dig about it, and dung it:

And if it bear fruit, well: and if not, then after that thou shalt cut it down.

COMMENTARY

Addressed to the disciples, this parable teaches the necessity of repentance but also suggests the effort and patience that will be required of them in their mission to help sinners to repent.

Returning to the agricultural metaphors of earlier parables, the fig tree here represents a sinful person, while the act of bearing fruit is symbolic of repentance. The setting evokes the Old Testament concept of Israel as God's vineyard, but the intercession of the gardener introduces a note of leniency consistent with Luke's milder, more humane approach. However, although the fig tree is given a year in which to prove itself, failure to produce fruit will result in its destruction. Jesus prefaced this parable with an even more explicit warning to his apostles about repentance, reminding them of the grisly fates of some of their fellow countrymen, who were massacred, crushed to death, etc., and adding, "But except ye repent, ye shall likewise perish."

THE PARABLE OF THE WEDDING GUEST

LUKE 14:7–11

And he put forth a parable to those which were bidden, when he marked how they chose out the chief rooms; saying unto them,

When thou art bidden of any man to a wedding, sit not down in the highest room; lest a more honorable man than thou be bidden of him;

And he that bade thee and him come and say to thee, Give this man place; and thou begin with shame to take the lowest room.

But when thou art bidden, go and sit down in the lowest room; that when he that bade thee cometh, he may say unto thee, Friend, go up higher: then shalt thou have worship in the presence of them that sit at meat with thee.

For whosoever exalteth himself shall be abased; and he that humbleth himself shall be exalted.

COMMENTARY

Like the Parable of the Great Supper, which it precedes, this story centers around a feast and involves a reversal in the guest list (and specifically in the seating arrangements). Luke tells us that both parables were addressed to an audience of lawyers and Pharisees, who had been invited along with him to a meal at the chief Pharisee's house. The parable's allusion to a wedding celebration, whose host can pick and choose guests at his discretion, is an effective reminder of God's power to select candidates for his kingdom. Using the image of a shaming social faux pas, Jesus warns against self-aggrandizement, such as that of the Pharisees who expected to be rewarded for their righteousness, and demonstrates that humility (such as exemplified in his own life and death) is more esteemed in the kingdom of heaven.

LUKE 14:28–30

For which of you, intending to build a tower, sitteth not down first, and counteth the cost, whether he have sufficient to finish it?

Lest haply, after he hath laid the foundation, and is not able to finish it, all that behold it begin to mock him.

Saying, This man began to build, and was not able to finish.

THE PARABLE OF THE WARRING KING

LUKE 14:31–33

Or what king, going to make war against another king, sitteth not down first, and consulteth whether he be able with ten thousand to meet him that cometh against him with twenty thousand?

Or else, while the other is yet a great way off, he sendeth an ambassage, and desireth conditions of peace?

So likewise, whosoever he be of you that forsaketh not all that he hath, he cannot be my disciple.

COMMENTARY

Turning his attention from the Pharisees, Jesus used this pair of stories, spoken to a large crowd, to make the point that following God was likely to be fraught with difficulty and should not to be undertaken lightly. The two stories describe considerable human ventures, the first—expensive building work subject to the scrutiny of critical neighbors—drawn from the domestic sphere, the second, a scene of violence describing the politicking of international warfare. With the odds similarly stacked against them, God's followers need total commitment, in which even family obligations would have to be set aside, as Jesus made clear moments earlier: "If any man come to me, and hate not his father, and mother, and wife, and children, and brethren, and sister, yea, and his own life also, he cannot be my disciple."

LUKE 15:8–10

Either what woman having ten pieces of silver, if she lose one piece, doth not light a candle, and sweep the house, and seek diligently till she find it?

And when she hath found it, she calleth her friends and her neighbors together, saying, Rejoice with me; for I have found the piece which I had lost.

Likewise, I say unto you, there is joy in the presence of the angels of God over one sinner that repenteth.

COMMENTARY

The second in Luke's trilogy of parables about lost things, this story has a domestic setting and is one of only a few parables in which the main character is a woman. As in the Parable of the Lost Sheep, the "loser" abandons everything to look for the lost item—Luke's housewife even lights a candle to meticulously search the dark corners of her house. In all three parables Luke carefully records the emotion experienced at the moment of finding; the achievement is an unreservedly joyful one, an event worthy of celebration, to be shared with friends and neighbors. With its homely imagery and heartwarming denouement, the parable shows its audience the importance of individual sinners who repent—a typically Lukan message of reassurance and optimism.

THE PARABLE OF THE PRODIGAL SON

LUKE 15:11–32

And he said, A certain man had two sons:

And the younger of them said to his father, Father, give me the portion of goods that falleth to me. And he divided unto them his living.

And not many days after the younger son gathered all together, and took his

---

DOMENICO FETTI, *THE PARABLE OF THE LOST PENCE*
before 1621, oil on poplar wood
Staatliche Kunstsammlungen Dresden

The overturned stool, upended basket, and rummaged-through linen chest testify to the intensity of the woman's search. She pauses only to light a lamp, to illuminate her sparsely furnished room, before continuing her quest.

LUCA GIORDANO, *THE PRODIGAL SON*
seventeenth century, oil
Photo: National Trust Photographic Library/Prudence Cuming

TAKING LEAVE OF HIS FATHER

The prodigal has demanded his share of the inheritance, and while his father's household busy themselves with coffers and calculations, the young heir leans impatiently on the table, clutching a bag of money in his hand. His leave-taking is a cursory affair: the prodigal can hardly wait to be on his way.

journey into a far country, and there wasted his substance with riotous living.

And when he had spent all, there arose a mighty famine in that land; and he began to be in want.

And he went and joined himself to a citizen of that country; and he sent him into his fields to feed swine.

And he would fain have filled his belly with the husks that the swine did eat: and no man gave unto him.

RIOTOUS LIVING

The prodigal wastes no time in dissipating himself and his wealth on idle pleasures and paid companions.

And when he came to himself, he said, How many hired servants of my father's have bread enough and to spare, and I will perish with hunger!

I will arise and go to my father, and will say unto him, Father, I have sinned against heaven, and before thee,

And am no more worthy to be called thy son: make me as one of thy hired servants.

And he arose, and came to his father. But when he was yet a great way off, his father saw him, and had compassion, and ran, and fell on his neck, and kissed him.

And the son said unto him, Father, I have sinned against heaven, and in thy sight, and am no more worthy to be called thy son.

But the father said to his servants, Bring forth the best robe, and put it on him; and put a ring on his hand, and shoes on his feet:

DRIVEN OUT BY HIS EMPLOYERS

When his money runs out, so does the friendship of his erstwhile companions. The prodigal is ignominiously chased out of town, in an episode not recorded in Luke's account of the parable.

And bring hither the fatted calf, and kill it; and let us eat and be merry.

Now his elder son was in the field: and as he came and drew nigh to the house, he heard musick and dancing.

And he called one of the servants, and asked him what these things meant.

And he said unto him, Thy brother is come; and thy father hath killed the fatted calf, because he hath received him safe and sound.

And he was angry, and would not go in: therefore came his father out, and intreated him.

And he answering said to his father, Lo, these many years do I serve thee, neither transgressed I at any time thy commandment: and yet thou never gavest me a kid, that I might make merry with my friends:

THE PENITENT SWINEHERD

Against the backdrop of a stormy landscape, the prodigal makes his life-changing decision: "I will arise and go to my father, and will say unto him, Father, I have sinned against heaven, and before thee."

But as soon as this thy son was come, which hath devoured thy living with harlots, thou hast killed for him the fatted calf.

And he said unto him, Son, thou art ever with me, and all that I have is thine.

It was meet that we should make merry, and be glad: for this thy brother was dead, and is alive again; and was lost, and is found.

COMMENTARY

The climax of Luke's sequence of "lost and found" parables, the Prodigal Son's extended narrative (the longest of all Jesus' parables) recounts the loss and return not of a possession—a sheep or a coin—but of a beloved family member. Sharing the strong

RECEIVED HOME BY HIS FATHER

The prodigal's father hastens out of the house to welcome his penitent son.

---

characterization common to Luke's parables, the Prodigal Son, like the parables of the Good Samaritan and the Rich Man and Lazarus, strikes us as being a story about real people. The feckless son, the obedient but resentful older brother, the indulgent father are all vivid portraits that encourage audience identification.

Told by Jesus on his final, fateful journey to Jerusalem, this parable is, along with that of the Unjust Steward, one of his last calls to repentance. While it is primarily the story of a penitent son, the unquestioning, all-encompassing forgiveness of the father also provides a metaphor for divine compassion. Clearly it is more extensive than the parables of the Lost Sheep and the Lost Coin, but Luke controls the narrative just as scrupulously; the double reversal of the younger son's fortunes—from well-to-do heir to swineherd, via the high life and famine, to long-lost son—is swiftly recounted, al-

THE FATTED CALF

In spite of the older brother's objections, a feast marks the return of the son who "was dead, and is alive again; and was lost, and is found."

lowing Luke to dwell on the son's repentance and his homecoming. The father's welcome is lavish, with the ring and new robes signifying re-absorption into the family fold. The extravagance of the celebrations provide a counterpoint to how utterly the younger son has transgressed. The young man's prodigality is comprehensively established by Luke—he distances himself geographically and spiritually from his home, he wastes his inheritance, and by working for a Gentile and looking after unclean animals, he falls foul of Jewish laws; he becomes, in fact, no better than a tax collector. Seen in this light, his prodigious welcome home would have been unsettling, if not shocking, to Jesus' original audience.

The younger brother's willingness to repent and to humble himself in front of his father is contrasted with his older brother's petulant refusal to join the feast and his ready bad-mouthing of his younger sibling; some commentators have discerned in this an allegory of the old Jewish religion and Christianity. The older brother, jealous and resentful of the welcome accorded to his wayward younger sibling, complains to his father that his own goodness has never been rewarded—an attitude emblematic of the Pharisees' self-righteousness and their resistance to Jesus' mission. The younger brother, a sinner who repents and finds favor with his father, has in turn been seen as representative of the new (Christian) Church.

The parable ends on an optimistic note despite the older brother's churlishness and stresses the joy that accompanies the prodigal's return. The story concludes with a celebratory meal—a mirror of Jesus' own table-fellowship with sinners and of the Communion, his "new Testament"—and the father justifies his decision to celebrate the return of his son, managing, like most parents, to have the last word.

THE PARABLE OF THE UNJUST STEWARD

LUKE: 16:1–13

And he said also unto his disciples, There was a certain rich man, which had a steward; and the same was accused unto him that he had wasted his goods.

And he called him, and said unto him, How is it that I hear this of thee? give me an account of thy stewardship; for thou mayest be no longer steward.

Then the steward said within himself, What shall I do? for my lord taketh away from me the stewardship: I cannot dig; to beg I am ashamed.

I am resolved what to do, that, when I am put out of the stewardship, they may receive me into their houses.

So he called every one of his lord's debtors unto him, and said unto the first, How much owest thou unto my lord?

And he said, An hundred measures of oil. And he said unto him, Take thy bill, and sit down quickly, and write fifty.

Then said he to another, And how much owest thou? And he said, An hundred measures of wheat. And he said unto him, Take thy bill, and write fourscore.

And the lord commended the unjust steward, because he had done wisely: for the children of this world are in their generation wiser than the children of light.

And I say unto you, Make to yourselves friends of the mammon of unrighteousness; that, when ye fail, they may receive you into everlasting habitations.

He that is faithful in that which is least is faithful also in much: and he that is unjust in the least is unjust also in much.

If therefore ye have not been faithful in the unrighteous mammon, who will commit to your trust the true riches?

And if ye have not been faithful in that which is another man's, who shall give you that which is your own?

No servant can serve two masters: for either he will hate the one and love the other; or else he will hold to the one and despise the other. Ye cannot serve God and mammon.

COMMENTARY

Located immediately after the Parable of the Prodigal Son, this parable is less accessible than its more popular predecessor. The crux of the problem facing modern readers lies in the householder's hearty commendation of his steward's flagrantly amoral behavior. The association made—by virtue of other parables—of the householder as God and the servants as God's followers makes the scenario even more baffling. The succession of conflicting and confusing applications—no fewer than six—tagged on at the end of the story testify to the difficulties encountered by earlier commentators. None of these statements, although expressing worthy sentiments, are entirely applicable to the narrative of the parable—some indeed seem more appropriate to other servant/master parables, such as that of the Talents/Pounds.

In order to read the parable coherently, it is necessary to ignore these applications and to concentrate on the story itself. The parable tells of a man on the make whose dishonesty has been discovered and who now stands to lose both his livelihood and his status. The steward's perilous situation demands drastic action; he has to act quickly and decisively. Contrary to our expectation, his reprehensible response is condoned—even applauded—by his employer. Jesus used this scenario to startle his audience into realizing that they, too, must acknowledge the serious situation that faces them. The crisis confronting them—the arrival of the kingdom of heaven—requires them to take bold action in order to save themselves, to make themselves acceptable when God calls them to account.

THE PARABLE OF THE RICH MAN AND LAZARUS

LUKE 16:19–31

There was a certain rich man, which was clothed in purple and fine linen, and fared sumptuously every day:

And there was a certain beggar named Lazarus, which was laid at his gate, full of sores,

JACOPO BASSANO, THE RICH MAN AND LAZARUS
c. 1554, oil on canvas
© The Cleveland Museum of Art, 1996, Delia E. and L. E. Holden Funds, 1939.68

And desiring to be fed with the crumbs which fell from the rich man's table: moreover the dogs came and licked his sores.

And it came to pass, that the beggar died, and was carried by the angels into Abraham's bosom: the rich man also died, and was buried;

And in hell he lift up his eyes, being in torments, and seeth Abraham afar off, and Lazarus in his bosom.

And he cried and said, Father Abraham, have mercy on me, and send Lazarus, that he may dip the tip of his finger in water, and cool my tongue; for I am tormented in this flame.

But Abraham said, Son, remember that thou in thy lifetime receivedst thy good things, and likewise Lazarus evil things: but now he is comforted, and thou art tormented.

And beside all this, between us and you there is a great gulf fixed: so that they which would pass from hence to you cannot; neither can they pass to us, that would come from thence.

Then he said, I pray thee therefore, father, that thou wouldest send him to my father's house:

For I have five brethren; that he may testify to them, lest they also come into this place of torment.

Abraham saith unto him, They have Moses and the prophets; let them hear them.

And he said, Nay, father Abraham: but if one went unto them from the dead, they will repent.

And he said unto them, If they hear not Moses and the prophets, neither will they be persuaded, though one rose from the dead.

COMMENTARY

Featuring a named character, the parable is unique among Jesus' parables and, as befits this particularized approach, is presented as a factual event rather than an allegory in which everything has an alternate meaning. Like other parables, however, the story pivots on the reversal of the two main characters' positions, and in fact the momentum of the story as a whole is built around a series of contrasts; thus, the Rich Man's wealth is juxtaposed with Lazarus' poverty, his huge meals with the crumbs Lazarus scavenges, heaven with hell, hot with cool, water with fire. As in the Parable of the Rich Fool, this story demonstrates the impermanence of wealth and its impotence in relation to the kingdom of heaven. Although the Rich Man (in some versions referred to as Dives, Latin for "rich man") has shown no mercy on Lazarus in his earthly life, he seems to expect a continuation of his privileges after death, assuming a right to receive mercy and for Moses and the prophets to help his brothers. The irrevocable reversal of the men's roles exemplifies the necessity of showing mercy to those less fortunate (a sentiment similar to that expressed in the Parable of the Great Supper, and one feels confident Lazarus would have been invited to that meal). Luke, however, doesn't lose sight of the realities of the kingdom—it is also a parable about the importance of obeying the law, echoing Jesus' message "And it is easier for heaven and earth to pass, than one tittle of the law to fail."

LUKE 18:1–8

And he spake a parable unto them to this end, that men ought always to pray, and not to faint;

Saying, There was in a city a judge, which feared not God, neither regarded man:

And there was a widow in that city; and she came unto him saying, Avenge me of mine adversary.

And he would not for a while: but afterward he said within himself, Though I fear not God, nor regard man;

Yet because this widow troubleth me, I will avenge her, lest by her continual coming she weary me.

And the Lord said, Hear what the unjust judge saith.

And shall not God avenge his own elect, which cry day and night unto him, though he bear long with them?

I tell you that he will avenge them speedily. Nevertheless when the Son of man cometh, shall he find faith on the earth?

COMMENTARY

This parable comes after Jesus' somewhat ominous description of his Second Coming at the end of the previous chapter, and strikes a more optimistic note after the portentous references to Sodom and Lot's wife. Jesus returns to the message of the Parable of the Friend at Midnight, using the triumph of the importunate widow over the powerful judge to reiterate the importance of perseverance and prayer. The parable is framed by Jesus' explanation and it carries a similar exemplum as the Parable of the Friend at Midnight, implying, "If this is how someone with no respect for anything reacts to the pleas of a humble widow, how much more will God respond to the continual prayers of his followers." The parable, unique to Luke's Gospel and perhaps included with the sufferings of the persecuted early Church in mind, also reflects Luke's interest in prayer, which is a significant element throughout his text—indeed, he records nine examples of Jesus' own prayers.

SIR JOHN EVERETT MILLAIS, *THE UNJUST JUDGE*
1864, wood engraving

One of Millais's more exotic parable compositions. With an airy wave of his hand, the hard-hearted judge dismisses the importunate widow, while his bodyguard tries to drag her away. A group of courtiers look on in amusement—one even peeks over the top of the judge's chair to get a better view.

THE PARABLE OF THE PHARISEE AND THE TAX COLLECTOR

LUKE 18:9–14

And he spake this parable unto certain which trusted in themselves that they were righteous, and despised others:

Two men went up into the temple to pray; the one a Pharisee, and the other a publican.

The Pharisee stood and prayed thus with himself, God, I thank thee, that I am not as other men are, extortioners, unjust, adulterers, or even as this publican.

I fast twice in the week, I give tithes of all that I possess.

And the publican, standing afar off, would not lift up so much as his eyes unto heaven, but smote upon his breast, saying, God be merciful to me a sinner.

I tell you, this man went down to his house justified rather than the other: for every one that exalteth himself shall be abased; and he that humbleth himself shall be exalted.

COMMENTARY

Having demonstrated the need for prayer, Jesus now provides an example of how to pray, and contrasts it with how not to pray. The parable recalls that of the Wedding Feast in both its conclusion and its role reversals of the humble and the (self) important. For its original audience the parable would have involved another, unusual reversal—that of their own expectations. Modern readers, hindered by the benefit of hindsight, have become accustomed to the once-shocking concepts of Pharisees as the villains of the piece and sinners as heroes. The Pharisees, with their careful observance of the religious laws, would have been admired and set the standard for emulation while publicans (tax collectors) were reviled as collaborators with the occupying Roman authorities and were widely regarded as crooks. As in the Parable of the Good Samaritan, Jesus used shock tactics to provoke his audience into rethinking the status quo and realizing that their relationship with God cannot be determined by their own sense of merit.

SIR JOHN EVERETT MILLAIS, *THE PHARISEE AND THE PUBLICAN*
1864, wood engraving

Berating himself for his unworthiness, the tax collector shields himself from the rest of the congregation by standing behind a pillar. Among the worshipers we see the haughtily upright figure of the Pharisee, exalting himself before God.

MINOR PARABLES

THE BRIDEGROOM'S GUESTS

MARK 2:19–20

And Jesus said unto them, Can the children of the bridechamber fast, while the bridegroom is with them? as long as they have the bridegroom with them, they cannot fast.

But the days will come, when the bridegroom shall be taken away from them, and then shall they fast in those days.

MATTHEW 9:15

And Jesus said unto them, Can the children of the bridechamber mourn, as long as the bridegroom is with them? but the days will come, when the bridegroom shall be taken from them, and then shall they fast.

WILLIAM BLAKE, *THE WISE AND FOOLISH VIRGINS*
c. 1822, pen, Indian ink, gray wash, and watercolor
Fitzwilliam Museum, Cambridge

An angel overhead trumpets the Bridegroom's arrival. The Wise Virgins have lighted their lamps and stand in readiness. Their dignified composure highlights the disheveled appearance of their ill-prepared sisters, who sink to their knees and tear at their headdresses in dismay. One of the Wise Virgins points to the town on the horizon, indicating where the foolish should go to buy new supplies of oil.

And he said unto them, Can ye make the children of the bridechamber fast, while the bridegroom is with them?

But the days will come, when the bridegroom shall be taken away from them, and then shall they fast in those days.

THE STRONG MAN BOUND

MARK 3:27

No man can enter into a strong man's house, and spoil his goods, except he will first bind the strong man; and then he will spoil his house.

LUKE 11:21–23

When a strong man armed keepeth his palace, his goods are in peace:

But when stronger than he shall come upon him, and overcome him, he taketh from him all his armor wherein he trusted, and divideth his spoils.

He that is not with me is against me: and he that gathereth not with me scattereth.

THE LAMP AND MEASURE

MARK 4:21–25

And he said unto them, Is a candle brought to be put under a bushel, or under a bed? and not to be set on a candlestick?

For there is nothing hid, which shall not be manifested; neither was any thing kept secret, but that it should come abroad.

If any man have ears to hear, let him hear.

And he said unto them, Take heed what ye hear: with what measure ye mete, it shall be measured to you: and unto you that hear shall more be given.

For he that hath, to him shall be given: and he that hath not, from him shall be taken even that which he hath.

LUKE 8:16–18

No man, when he hath lighted a candle, covereth it with a vessel or putteth it under a bed; but setteth it on a candlestick, that they which enter in may see the light.

For nothing is secret, that shall not be made manifest; neither any thing hid, that shall not be known and come abroad.

Take heed therefore how ye hear: for whosoever hath, to him shall be given; and whosoever hath not, from him shall be taken even that which he seemeth to have.

FATHER AND CHILDREN'S REQUESTS

MATTHEW 7:9–11

Or what man is there of you, whom if his son ask bread, will he give him a stone?

Or if he ask fish, will he give him a serpent?

If ye then, being evil, know how to give good gifts unto your children, how much more shall your Father which is in heaven give good things to them that ask him?

LUKE 11:11–13

If a son shall ask bread of any of you that is a father, will he give him a stone? or if he ask a fish, will he for a fish give him a serpent?

Or if he shall ask an egg, will he offer him a scorpion?

If ye then, being evil, know how to give good gifts unto your children: how much more shall your heavenly Father give the Holy Spirit to them that ask him?

TWO WAYS / TWO DOORS

MATTHEW 7:13–14

Enter ye in at the strait gate: for wide is the gate, and broad is the way, that leadeth to destruction, and many there be which go in thereat:

Because strait is the gate, and narrow is the way, which leadeth unto life, and few there be that find it.

LUKE 13:24

Strive to enter in at the strait gate: for many, I say unto you, will seek to enter in, and shall not be able.

MATTHEW 7:16–20

Ye shall know them by their fruits. Do men gather grapes of thorns, or figs of thistles?

Even so every good tree bringeth forth good fruit; but a corrupt tree bringeth forth evil fruit.

A good tree cannot bring forth evil fruit, neither can a corrupt tree bring forth good fruit.

Every tree that bringeth not forth good fruit is hewn down, and cast into the fire.

Wherefore by their fruits ye shall know them.

SALT

LUKE 14:34–35

Salt is good: but if the salt have lost his savour, wherewith shall it be seasoned?

It is neither fit for the land, nor yet for the dunghill; but men cast it out. He that hath ears to hear, let him hear.

MARK 9:50

Salt is good: but if the salt have lost his saltness, wherewith shall ye season it? Have salt in yourselves, and have peace with one another.

HOUSEHOLDER

MATTHEW 13:52

Then said he unto them, Therefore every scribe which is instructed unto the kingdom of heaven is like unto a man that is an householder, which bringeth forth out of his treasure things new and old.

LUKE 17:7–10

But which of you having a servant plowing or feeding cattle, will say unto him by and by, when he is come from the field, Go and sit down to meat?

And will not rather say unto him, Make ready wherewith I may sup, and gird thyself, and serve me, till I have eaten and drunken; and afterward thou shalt eat and drink?

Doth he thank that servant because he did the things that were commanded him? I trow not.

So likewise ye, when ye shall have done all those things which are commanded you, say, We are unprofitable servants: we have done that which was our duty to do.

T H E   M O T E   A N D   T H E   B E A M

MATTHEW 7:1–5

Judge not, that ye be not judged.

For with what judgment ye judge, ye shall be judged: and with what measure ye mete, it shall be measured to you again.

And why beholdest thou the mote that is in thy brother's eye, but considerest not the beam that is in thine own eye?

Or how wilt thou say to thy brother, Let me pull out the mote out of thine eye; and, behold, a beam is in thine own eye?

Thou hypocrite, first cast out the beam out of thine own eye; and then shalt thou see clearly to cast the mote out of thy brother's eye.

LUKE 6:41–42

And why beholdest thou the mote that is in thy brother's eye, but perceivest not the beam that is in thine own eye?

Either how canst thou say to thy brother, Brother, let me pull out the mote that is in thine eye, when thou thyself beholdest not the beam that is in thine own eye? Thou hypocrite, cast out first the beam out of thine own eye, and then shalt thou see clearly to pull out the mote that is in thy brother's eye.

MATTHEW 15:12–14

Then came his disciples, and said unto him, Knowest thou that the Pharisees were offended, after they heard this saying?

But he answered and said, Every plant, which my heavenly Father hath not planted, shall be rooted up.

Let them alone: they be blind leaders of the blind. And if the blind lead the blind, both shall fall into the ditch.

LUKE 6:39

And he spake a parable unto them, Can the blind lead the blind? shall they not both fall into the ditch?

THE BUDDING FIG TREE

MATTHEW 24:32–36

Now learn a parable of the fig tree; When his branch is yet tender, and putteth forth leaves, ye know that summer is nigh:

So likewise ye, when ye shall see all these things, know that it is near, even at the doors.

Verily I say unto you, This generation shall not pass, till all these things be fulfilled.

Heaven and earth shall pass away, but my words shall not pass away.

But of that day and hour knoweth no man, no, not the angels of heaven, but my Father only.

PRECEDING PAGES: PIETER BREUGHEL THE ELDER, *THE BLIND LEADING THE BLIND*
1568, tempera on canvas
National Museum, Naples

The leading blind man has already tumbled into the ditch and is about to be joined by his fellow, who realizes his error too late. The rest of the processsion continue to follow one another unsuspectingly.

Now learn a parable of the fig tree; When her branch is yet tender, and putteth forth leaves, ye know that summer is near:

So ye in like manner, when ye shall see these things come to pass, know that it is night, even at the doors.

LUKE 21:29–33

And he spake to them a parable; Behold the fig tree, and all the trees;

When they now shoot forth, ye see and know of your own selves that summer is now nigh at hand.

Verily I say unto you, This generation shall not pass away, till all be fulfilled.

Heaven and earth shall pass away: but my words shall not pass away.

THE CHILDREN IN THE MARKETPLACE

MATTHEW 11:16–19

But whereunto shall I liken this generation? It is like unto children sitting in the markets, and calling unto their fellows,

And saying, We have piped unto you, and ye have not danced; we have mourned unto you, and ye have not lamented.

For John came neither eating nor drinking, and they say, He hath a devil.

The Son of man came eating and drinking, and they say, Behold a man gluttonous, and a winebibber, a friend of publicans and sinners. But wisdom is justified of her children.

LUKE 7:31–35

And the Lord said, Whereunto then shall I liken the men of this generation? and to what are they like?

They are like unto children sitting in the marketplace, and calling one to another, and saying, We have piped unto you, and ye have not danced; we have mourned to you, and ye have not wept.

For John the Baptist came neither eating bread nor drinking wine; and ye say, He hath a devil.

The Son of man is come eating and drinking; and ye say, Behold a gluttonous man, and a winebibber, a friend of publicans and sinners!

But wisdom is justified of all her children.

MATTHEW 25:31–33

When the Son of man shall come in his glory, and all the holy angels with him, then shall he sit upon the throne of his glory:

And before him shall be gathered all nations: and he shall separate them one from another, as a shepherd divideth his sheep from the goats:

And he shall set the sheep on his right hand, but the goats on the left.

DEFILEMENT

MARK 7:15

There is nothing from without a man, that entering into him can defile him: but the things which come out of him, those are they that defile the man.

JESUS' EXPLANATION OF THE PARABLE OF DEFILEMENT

MARK 7:17–23

And when he was entered into the house from the people, his disciples asked him concerning the parable.

And he saith unto them, Are ye so without understanding also? Do ye not perceive, that whatsoever thing from without entereth into the man, it cannot defile him;

Because it entereth not into his heart, but into the belly, and goeth out into the draught, purging all meats?

And he said, That which cometh out of the man, that defileth the man.

For from within, out of the heart of men, proceed evil thoughts, adulteries, fornications, murders.

Thefts, covetousness, wickedness, deceit, lasciviousness, an evil eye, blasphemy, pride, foolishness:

All these evil things come from within, and defile the man.

SIR JOHN EVERETT MILLAIS, *THE LOST SHEEP*
1864, wood engraving

THE PARABLES AND CHRISTIAN ART

For more than fifteen hundred years the history of Western art has been bound up with that of Christianity. It is hard to imagine how European art would have developed had not Christianity existed, for as the Church expanded into a powerful and wealthy institution, it became one of the most important patrons of the arts. Early Christian art, however, was a more clandestine affair, and with little extant from the first three centuries after Jesus' death, its origins remain obscure. During its formative years Christianity was an illegal religion and its followers subject to hostility and oppression. Against a background of intolerance, Christian worship literally went underground. The networks of subterranean chambers where the Christians buried their dead doubled up as miniature churches and provided sanctuary in times of persecution. Despite the dark, cramped conditions, the walls of these cemeteries (known as "catacombs") were decorated with paintings—the oldest surviving examples of Christian art. Often crudely executed and now fragmented with age, these murals nevertheless yield important information about the emergence of Christian iconography.

Early Christians were clearly keen to express their faith visually, but as followers of a new religion, they lacked ready-made imagery of their own. Despite the Second

---

THE GOOD SHEPHERD, CATACOMB PAINTING
third century A.D., fresco
Photo: Sonia Halliday Photographs, Photo by André Held

A popular subject in early Christian art, evocative of the Parable of the Lost Sheep, but more specifically illustrating Christ's words as recorded in John's Gospel: "I am the good shepherd: the good shepherd giveth his life for the sheep" (10:11).

Commandment's injunction against "graven images," figurative art was not unknown in Judaism. Extensive frescoes of Old Testament subjects discovered in a third-century synagogue in Syria have been cited as evidence that Jewish art could have been an influence. The Old Testament remained a source of inspiration for Christian artists, but their catacomb paintings of stories like Daniel in the Lions' Den and Jonah and the Whale contain a distinctive subtext, obliquely articulating Christian suffering and hopes of redemption. Although the two religions were closely associated in the first centuries A.D., Christian art drew much of its style and substance not from Jewish art but from the readily accessible pagan art of the Roman Empire. Popular in classical art and literature, pastoral subjects in particular proved themselves pliant prototypes, well suited to the rural symbolism of Christianity. The Good Shepherd is a recurrent image in the catacombs, watching over his flock or, as in the third-century painting in the Lucine Crypt of Rome's Callisto Cemetery, carrying a sheep on his shoulder, as described in Luke's Parable of the Lost Sheep. Conspicuously absent from this evolving iconography was the image that, in later art, would epitomize Christ's suffering and sacrifice: the Crucifixion itself. A form of execution reserved for the worst criminals, the crucifixion was a source of shame for early Christians and did not appear in their art until the fifth century.

Found under cities throughout the Roman Empire—in Asia Minor, North Africa, as well as in Italy—the catacombs feature the first known parable paintings. The Coemeterium Maius in Rome contains a mural of the Wise Virgins, an appropriately eschatological choice by a community preoccupied by death and the imminence of the Last Judgment. The presence of the Wise Virgins, with their lamps lit and held aloft in readiness to attend a banquet, suggests, nevertheless, a certain optimism, a visualization of the community's prayers that the departed might, too, have been admitted to God's heavenly feast. The practice of catacomb burial declined with the legalization of Christianity in the fourth century, and Christians increasingly began to bury their dead in sarcophagi. Low-relief carvings on the sides of these stone or marble coffins contain the earliest portrayals of Christ and his Apostles. A fifth-century stone sarcophagus shares the funerary concerns of catacomb paintings but expresses the desire for salvation by depicting one of Christ's miracles—Lazarus being raised from the dead. The sculpture illustrates another problem encountered by early Christian artists, namely how to portray Jesus. The Messiah's appearance had gone unrecorded in the Gospels and neither, it seems, had any contemporary portraits been made of him. In the absence of source material artists turned again to the pagan art of Rome, basing their Christ figure on that of Apollo, the classical god of sun and light. Apollo was also regarded as an ideal of male beauty and Christian artists absorbed this tradition, depicting Jesus as a clean-shaven, short-haired, athletic young man, wearing (as in the sarcophagus relief) a Roman toga.

Christian art was able to get into its stride when the Roman emperor Constantine adopted Christianity as the state religion in A.D. 312. Officially sanctioned, Christian art became public art for the first time, no longer relegated to underground tombs and coffins. New places of worship were built, among them the basilica of St. Peter's in Rome, which was dedicated in A.D. 326, and later former pagan temples were appropriated for Christian use. Christian art quickly set about educating as well as inspiring its audience, the adoption of classical art and architecture no doubt allowing the new religion to be more readily accepted by the populace. In spite of the reservations expressed by some early Church fathers, Saint Augustine among them, Christian art flourished, and by the end of the fourth century it had become common for churches to be extensively adorned with narrative and symbolic representations.

JESUS RAISES LAZARUS, SARCOPHAGUS SCULPTURE
fifth century A.D., stone
Photo: © Sonia Halliday Photographs

This low-relief carving closely adheres to John's account of Jesus' miracle: "And he that was dead came forth, bound hand and foot with grave-clothes: and his face was bound about with a napkin" (11:44).

Having embraced Christianity, it was not long before Constantine made another momentous decision. Barely two decades later, in A.D. 330, he transferred the capital of his empire from Rome to Byzantium, modestly renaming the city after himself—Constantinople. The upheaval had far-reaching effects, not least on the style and iconography of Christian art. Until then primarily a fusion of Greek and Roman style, Christian art was now exposed to Eastern aesthetics, a collision of cultures that in turn spawned the Byzantine style. Distinct from the flowing, essentially naturalistic approach of its Roman predecessor, Byzantine art is characterized by its stiff, formalized figures and a hieratic approach somewhat akin to Egyptian art. As in classical art, considerable attention was paid to drapery, but Byzantine art rendered the intricate folds in a highly stylized, non-illusionistic manner. More significantly, Byzantine art endowed Christian iconography with an alternative "type" of Christ, which would eventually become the prevailing image of Jesus in subsequent centuries. The elegant Apollo type was supplemented by a bearded, long-haired figure whose dark, Eastern features exuded power and spirituality and who was often portrayed in his role as "Christ Pantocrator"—Christ, Creator of the Universe.

Much Byzantine church decoration took the form of mosaics, an ancient technique for surface decoration, using thousands of tiny cubes of stone or glass laid into cement to make up the picture or pattern. Mosaic was well suited to the Byzantine style and had the added attraction of extreme durability. Paradoxically, however, some of the best-known Byzantine mosaics are not in Constantinople but in the Italian city of Ravenna. Designated the capital of the Western Roman Empire in the early fifth century, Ravenna underwent an extensive building program during the emperor Justinian's reign and mosaics such as *The Good Shepherd* date from this period. The confident, balanced composition, vivid color, and elaborate decorative work of this mosaic make a telling contrast to the depiction of the same subject in the catacombs. The Good Shepherd is identified as Christ by his golden halo and the cross he holds in place of a shepherd's staff, his authority emphasized by his flock, who all look obediently at him. This Christ, beardless but with long dark hair, does not confirm entirely with either "type" of Jesus but is instead a compromise between the two.

The Roman Empire was permanently divided into two toward the end of the fourth century, heralding the decline of the western half. The eventual occupation of Rome by the Goths and the abdication of the last Roman emperor, Romulus Augustus, marked the end of the Empire and the onset of the Dark Ages. The Eastern Empire, by contrast, remained relatively cohesive and its stability was reflected in the longevity of the Byzantine style, which, despite a period of iconoclasm during the seventh and eighth centuries (during which representation of the human figure was forbidden), remained a potent influence on European art until the Renaissance.

During this period of disintegration and turmoil in Western Europe, monastic orders acted as guardians of the Christian faith, its traditions, and its art. Monasteries were

THE GOOD SHEPHERD, GALLA PLACIDA, RAVENNA
fifth century A.D., mosaic
Photo: © Sonia Halliday Photographs

"I am the good shepherd, and know my sheep, and am known of mine" (John 10:14).

important centers of scholarship, and the illuminations that adorned the manuscripts produced by the monks played a vital role in perpetuating Christian iconography. Like so many other aspects of European art, the practice of illustrating Christian texts had classical antecedents. Archaeological evidence and the testimony of ancient authors indicate that papyrus scrolls were sometimes illustrated and that scientific texts such as herbals would have been accompanied by explanatory drawings. The extensive narratives of epic poems such as the Iliad and Odyssey and, later, the Aeneiad offered greater artistic potential for illustrators and in turn provided a model for illustrations in Bible texts. Papyrus scrolls were superseded by the modern book format (or *codex*) by the fourth century, but the practice of illustration continued. Initially only individual books from the Bible such as Genesis were illuminated, but by the turn of the first millennium, Gospel Books were relatively common.

Intended for use on the church altar as the focal point of the service, Gospel Books tended to be large-scale productions, comprising the text of one or more of the Gospels, together with illustrations and often elaborate decorative work. The earliest known representation of the Parable of the Good Samaritan occurs in the Rossano Gospels, a sixth-century manuscript of Byzantine origin. The illustrations, stylistically influenced by mosaic and fresco art, include events from the life of Christ as well as a scene from the Parable of the Wise and Foolish Virgins. As Tintoretto would do a thousand years later (see p. 61), the manuscript artist depicts the climax of the parable, the moment when the Foolish Virgins, having gone away and bought oil for their lamps, return to ask the Bridegroom to let them into the wedding banquet. The Wise Virgins have already passed through the doorway now barred by the Bridegroom and are in heaven, shown here not as a banquet but as a beautiful landscape with verdant fruit trees and a clear, fast-flowing stream. Their purity and heavenly status is apparent also from their resplendent white and gold robes, so unlike the garish colors worn by their foolish sisters. The figure of Jesus appears in each of the Rossano Gospels' parable pictures—the heads of the Bridegroom and the Good Samaritan are encircled with a golden halo, clearly denoting their divine status.

Illuminated manuscripts and Gospel Books were produced all over Europe and

THE WISE AND FOOLISH VIRGINS, ROSSANO GOSPEL
sixth century A.D., manuscript
Museo Diocesano Arte Sacra

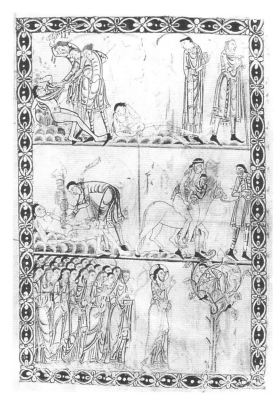

THE PARABLE OF THE GOOD SAMARITAN, THE BURY GOSPELS
twelfth century, manuscript
Photo: The Conway Library, Courtauld Institute of Art, reproduced by
permission of the Master and Fellows of Pembroke College, Cambridge

An illustration of the tax collector Zacchaeus, who climbed up into a tree to get a better view of Jesus, follows the story of the Good Samaritan.

different schools of illustration emerged, although there was considerable overlapping of style. Manuscripts like the twelfth-century Bury Gospels and fourteenth-century Holkham Bible Book show how adept artists became in conveying narrative through a few well-chosen images. The Bury Gospels' illustration of the Parable of the Good Samaritan is ruthlessly concise, recounting only the main events of the story: the attack on the traveler, the callous behavior of the Priest and Levite, the Good Samaritan's compassionate care of the wounded man, and (concluding with) the rescue party making their way to the inn (the rest of the page deals with the story of the tax collector Zacchaeus). As in modern-day cartoon strips, Bible illustrators used a linear style and format to convey narrative and, sharing their twentieth-century counterparts' need to sustain the

The Parable of the Wicked Husbandmen / The Stone That the Builders Rejected / The Parable of the Wedding Feast, Holkham Bible Book
(Add. MS. 47682)
fourteenth century, manuscript
By permission of The British Library

❧

Although restricted by the confines of the page, the artist vividly re-creates these two parables. We witness the treacherous machinations of the Wicked Tenants and the cold-blooded murder of the heir in the vineyard. We see, too, the decisive punishment of the improperly dressed wedding guest and the magnanimity of the King who invites the disabled and disadvantaged to his feast.

viewers' attention, often focused on dramatic, violent action. The illustrations that accompany the parables of the Wedding Feast and the Wicked Tenants in the Bury Gospels are even more concise: we simply see the improperly dressed guest being ignominiously ejected from the feast and witness the son of the vineyard owner being beaten to death.

An increase in book production followed in the wake of monastic reforms in the early Middle Ages as new orders were founded and more scribes became available. By the end of the twelfth century, however, book production began to pass from the scriptoria of the monasteries to lay artists. The rise of universities such as Oxford and Cambridge (founded in the twelfth and thirteenth centuries, respectively) led to greater numbers of literate laymen whose requirements of religious texts differed from those of ecclesiastical scholars. Books became smaller, as did the illustrations within them, reflecting their new function as personal possessions. The didactic element in religious texts, however, was ever present and illustrated Bibles, whose extensive illustrations helped to explain the text to lay readers, became popular. The moralizing nature of the parables complemented the educational endeavors of such books, and particularly dynamic parable illustrations can be found in the fourteenth-century manuscript, the so-called Holkham Bible Book. Unusually, its depiction of the Parable of the Wicked Husbandmen includes Christ's reference to the stone that the builders rejected, which is illustrated in a scene of medieval construction workers on a building site. The builders are equipped with the tools of their trade—mallet, mason's square, and plumb line—and they are engrossed in their work, unaware of the preceding scene of slaughter. The expulsion of the wedding guest without a garment follows this episode, the imperious pointing gesture of the host mirroring that of the father in the earlier parable. The illustrations dominate the page but explanatory texts have been provided, written in Anglo-Norman, the language of the upper-class laity in England at that time.

The audience for such books, however, was limited; the monied and literate were a minority, and it was art in churches that continued to supplement the religious education and spiritual nourishment of the illiterate majority. The legacy of Christian art had survived not only in monastic manuscripts but also in the sculpture and paintings in their churches. Figurative decoration in churches had early on become quite schematized—rigidly so in the Byzantine church—and particular scenes or events tended to be located in the same place. The west end of the building was associated with the future and accordingly often featured a depiction of the Last Judgment; the roof was symbolic of heaven and ceiling bosses sometimes contained illustrations of heavenly events such as the Coronation of the Virgin; and the nave was linked with the laity who worshipped there and so was regarded as a suitable place for instructive and inspirational subjects like the life of Christ. Parables, too, had their place in church art, and one of the most commonly represented parables of the Middle Ages was that of the Wise and Foolish Virgins. Retaining their association with the Last Judgment, the Virgins were often included in sculpted decoration around church doorways. Combined with the symbolism of the doorway, with its echoes of Jesus' assertion "I am the Way," the Virgins reminded worshippers as they entered the church that the Way had been denied to the Foolish ones. The Wise Virgins were sometimes linked with the glorification of the Virgin Mary and the Virgins who appear in the Doorway of the Betrothed at St. Sebald in Nuremberg teach young couples about marriage, not the Last Judgment. Nevertheless, the fundamental iconography of the parable had been firmly established. The Wise and Foolish Virgins were differentiated by their attributes, the empty, inverted lamps of the foolish and the raised, lighted lamps of the wise. The modest costumes, neat headdresses, and calm demeanor of the Wise Virgins also contrasted with the low-cut gowns, unpinned hair, and distraught poses of their foolish siblings.

The parable of the Rich Man [Dives] and Lazarus was also associated with the Last Judgment, and a sculpture of the story appears, appropriately, on the West Front of Lincoln Cathedral in England. At Moissac Abbey in France, the parable was interpreted as a story about Christian charity. The sculpted panels were placed on the western side of the south porch, the very place where mendicants would beg for alms. Working from right to left, the relief sculptures unflinchingly narrate the parallel lives of the two men. The Rich Man feasts with his wife, and while dogs at the foot of the table enthusiastically dine on Lazarus' sores, an angel carries Lazarus' soul to heaven, where he is pictured in Abraham's bosom, a symbol of paradise. Seated next to Abraham is Moses, who holds a scroll denoting the Law. In the larger lower panels, Dives' grisly death and punishment in hell offers a visual paraphrase of the Last Judgment and teaches a stark lesson about the fate of the uncharitable. As was common in medieval iconography, the sculpture highlights Dives' greed—on his deathbed a weighty money bag hangs from his neck to show that the mortal sin of avarice is the cause of his downfall.

The thoroughgoing program of religious instruction in medieval church art and architecture was noted by Victor Hugo, who remarked, "Human kind conceived of nothing in the middle ages which it did not write in stone." He might well have added "in glass," for it was during the thirteenth century, the age of the Gothic cathedrals in Northern Europe, that the art of stained glass rose to its zenith. Ecclesiastical power shifted away from the abbeys and monasteries and centered instead around the large churches that began to be built within the cities. As much an expression of civic pride as they were monuments to God's glory, cathedrals were built on a grand scale, often, as at Chartres (1194–1221), with considerable manual labor on the part of the townsfolk. The sheer size of these new buildings offered unprecedented scope for decoration that would inspire and instruct the densely populated cathedral congregations. Thanks to innovative construction techniques such as flying buttresses, windows could be made bigger than previously possible and, seizing the opportunity, cathedral planners filled the panels with jewel-colored picture stories from the Bible, apocrypha, and legends of the saints. So comprehensive were the decorative schemes of sculpture and painted glass that cathedrals came to be seen as "Bibles of the poor," enlightening worshippers spiritually and literally.

It is perhaps no surprise, then, that the layout of many stained-glass windows should resemble those Bible illustrations in which each episode was placed within a circular or quatrefoil medallion, a sequence of which made up the whole story and was encapsu-

THE PARABLE OF DIVES AND LAZARUS, MOISSAC ABBEY
twelfth century, stone carving
The Conway Library, Courtauld Institute of Art

The parable's narrative runs from right to left, starting at the upper-right corner of the porchway and concluding in the lower-left panel with a grisly depiction of the punishment of Avarice.

lated in the larger frame of the window or page. As in contemporary manuscripts, the artists approached their subject matter typologically, interpreting the events of the New Testament in the light of the Old. The Glossa Ordinaria, a tenth-century compilation of traditional allegorical explanations of the Bible, was a useful source for artists, but typology was still topical three centuries later and there was no shortage of contemporary debate from which medieval artists could draw. But in England, at least, echoes of earlier theologians' mistrust of religious imagery still reverberated. Critical of the "not only vain but even profane" work of some church artists, the author of the twelfth-century tract *Pictor in Carmine* advocated strictly religious themes for church paintings and even provided a list of some 650 types from which artists could choose.

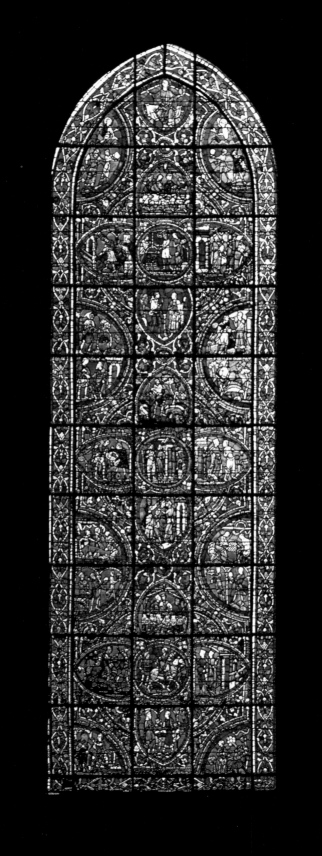

Canterbury Cathedral once contained a sequence of twelve typological windows, which, although not extant, were described in manuscripts that have survived. Divided into three main groups, the windows told the story of Christ's early life, his ministry, and his Passion. The scheme seems to have been influenced by a variety of sources, including the *Pictor in Carmine,* but differs from it by including parables in three of the windows of the ministry. Only two parable scenes remain, the Sower on stony ground with birds and the Sower on thorny and good ground (see pp. 24 and 28). Unusual in Western art at that time, the parable was given two "types": The Three Righteous Men (Daniel, Job, and Noah) represented the good ground, while the double portrait of Emperor Julian the Apostate (who renounced Christianity) and Maurice Tiberius personified men "choked by the cares of riches" and were emblematic of the thorny ground. Although the Good Samaritan featured in the scheme, other less widely represented parables, such as those of the Leaven, the Dragnet, and the Unmerciful Servant, were apparently included, along with a rare post–early Christian depiction of the Good Shepherd. The choice of parables underscored the eschatological themes of the scheme as a whole, the Good Samaritan additionally illustrating the Christian condemnation of the Jews' rejection of Jesus.

Parable subjects were popular on both sides of the Channel. At Chartres Cathedral the Good Samaritan was combined with the story of Adam and Eve and interpreted as an allegory of man's fall and redemption. Beginning with Jesus telling the parable to a group of Pharisees (see frontispiece), the window's narrative shows the traveler setting out from Jerusalem, whose "type," Adam and Eve being expelled from Eden, appears in the upper half of the window. In this interpretational scheme, the priest and Levite hastening past the wounded traveler represent the Old Testament and its failings, while the Samaritan is Christ, the savior. A more straightforward approach was adopted to recount the fall and redemption of the Prodigal Son. One of the earliest depictions of what would subsequently become the most frequently illustrated parable in art, the window in the north transept at Chartres (dated c. 1210) nevertheless narrates the story in detail. Considerable space (ten out of thirty panels) is devoted to showing the nature of the younger son's prodigality, with the artist extemporizing extra scenes to make explicit what Luke only inferred. Thus we see the prodigal "wasting his substance in riotous living," in whoring and gambling, before literally losing the shirt from his back

THE PARABLE OF THE PRODIGAL SON, WINDOW AT CHARTRES CATHEDRAL
c.1210, stained glass
Photo: Copyright Sonia Halliday and Laura Lushington

Apart from the additional scenes of the prodigal "wasting his substance," the window's thirty panels follow Luke's text. In the top panel sits Christ, flanked by two angels, his arms raised in benediction.

and being reduced to begging from his former companions. This emphasis later proved popular with artists in Northern Europe, in particular the Netherlands, who were were happy to relegate the less colorful elements of the story to the background or to treat the prodigal's debauchery as a subject in its own right.

The development of printing in fifteenth-century Europe also had a profound effect on the way Christian art was produced. Printing enabled the relatively quick and cheap production of multiple copies of texts and images, which could then be circulated among a wider audience. The German artist Albrecht Dürer did much to improve the quality and status of graphic art during the infancy of printing in the West. He produced numerous prints, both single images and series, on religious and other themes, of which *The Prodigal Son* (c. 1496) was one of the best known. Showing the repentant prodigal among the swine, the image was particularly popular in Italy, where it was praised in the sixteenth century by Giorgio Vasari, the biographer of Michelangelo.

Dürer himself had traveled in Italy in the early years of the sixteenth century and had experienced firsthand the art and architecture of the High Renaissance, the culmination of the revival and veneration for classical art and culture that had emerged in Italy at the beginning of the previous century. It was a period during which artists shook off the anonymity of the craftsman and created works of arts that even today can be attributed to named individuals. Artists mastered the laws of perspective and foreshortening, enabling them to attain new levels of naturalism—what the art historian Ernst Gombrich has called "the conquest of reality." Dürer was profoundly influenced by Italian Renaissance artists, notably Bellini and Leonardo da Vinci, whose scholarship in other areas, such as mathematics and geometry, he emulated on his return to Germany. Dürer's work was an important conduit of the ideas of the Renaissance and brought its humanist concerns to a Northern Europe whose art was characterized by a very different approach. Bosch's painting of *The Prodigal Son* (see p. 118) reflects the Northern artist's love of anecdotal, moralizing themes and a fondness for domestic subjects. The circular panel is crammed with detail, much of it symbolic. The physical dilapidation of the brothel—its broken windows, gaping roof, and crazily skewed shutter—points to the moral decay of its inhabitants, also evident in the assignation in the doorway and the man urinating at the side of the house. Unusually, Bosch depicts his prodigal beginning his journey home, and not at the moment of his spiritual awakening, although the prodigal's ragged clothes, mismatched footwear, and graying hair indicate the depths to which he has sunk. Appropriately, the inn sign seems to be a pelican—a symbol of penitence—while the presence of an owl, perched in the branches above the prodigal's head, acknowledges the wisdom of his decision.

During the religious struggles of the Reformation and Counter-Reformation that engulfed Europe in the sixteenth and seventeenth centuries, Christian art became increasingly politicized. In response to Protestant opposition to the papacy, the Roman Catholic Church sought to clarify and reaffirm its dogmas and doctrines. The official

Albrecht Dürer, *The Prodigal Son and the Swine*
c. 1496, engraving
Glasgow Museums, The Burrell Collection

Dürer's penitent prodigal kneels in prayer in a ramshackle farmyard. The image proved popular in Italy, its iconography prefiguring that later favored by the Catholic Church during the Counter-Reformation.

reforming party of the Catholic Church, the Council of Trent, was convened intermittently between 1545 and 1563 and its influence extended to artistic matters. Religious imagery came under official scrutiny and even well-known artists were not immune from censorship. In 1573 Veronese, the Venetian painter of biblical and historical subjects, was ordered by the Inquisition to alter or else destroy his portrayal of the Last Supper. His approach to the subject was deemed to have been profane and indecorous; nevertheless, a change of title ultimately saved the picture, and as *The Feast in the House of Levi,* Veronese's lively composition caused no offense.

HIERONYMOUS BOSCH, *THE PRODIGAL SON*
fifteenth/sixteenth century, oil on panel
Museum Boijmans Van Beuningen, Rotterdam

His fortunes at a nadir, the prodigal leaves his former playground, his worldly possessions now simply contained in a wicker basket strapped to his back.

The moralizing intent of Jesus' parables made them ideal fodder for religious propaganda on both sides, and prints of them were popularized by Protestants in the sixteenth century and Jesuits in the seventeenth. Typological interpretation was replaced by a more personal dynamic in which the individual's relationship with God was central. Jacopo Bassano's *Good Samaritan* (see p. 67) portrays the Samaritan simply as a compassionate human being responding to the need of a fellowman, whose wounded body is painted with gruesome realism. The artist includes a portrait of his hometown, Bassano, in the background, as if to reinforce the earthly dimension of the scene. The immediacy of Bassano's art resurfaces in another parable subject—*The Rich Man and Lazarus* (see p. 84). The painting seems curiously modern in its haunting evocation of an individual's alienation in society. The page boy stands alone, eyes downcast, lost in thought, oblivious to Lazarus, who lies prone on the floor, too weak to shoo away the predatory dogs. Even the Rich Man's feast is a somber affair: The table is devoid of food and the musician, lute idle in his hands, sits with his back to us, excluding the viewer in the same way Lazarus is shunned. Both parables explore the theme of Christian charity—a popular concept with both sides of the religious divide. As in earlier Christian art, the siting of sculpture or paintings added resonance to their pictorial content, and the Parable of the Good Samaritan was considered to be an appropriate subject for hospitals. The stairway of the Great Hall at St. Bartholomew's Hospital in London still features two murals by William Hogarth—one of Christ healing the paralytic at the pool at Bethesda, the other of the Good Samaritan looking after the wounded traveler. Murillo's *Return of the Prodigal Son* (see p. 18) was originally painted for the Hospital de la Caridad, a charitable foundation in Seville of which Murillo was a member. One of a series of seven works illustrating the Seven Corporeal Works of Mercy (as outlined by Jesus in Matthew 25:35–45), *The Prodigal Son* represented the charitable act of clothing the poor (Murillo included the pool at Bethesda to illustrate the tending of the sick). While the errant son, dressed in the tattered remnants of once-fine robes, his feet dirty and bare, falls to his knees to beg his father's forgiveness, servants emerge from the house bringing him new clothes, shoes, and even a ring. The more usual interpretation of the parable is not overlooked, though, and a calf being led in by a smiling child reminds us of the celebratory feast yet to come.

The Prodigal Son carried additional significance in Counter-Reformation iconography, for, affirming the sacrament of Penance as a prerequisite for salvation, the Council of Trent had in 1566 recommended the Prodigal Son as an exemplary Christian penitent. Artists now focused on the penitence of the prodigal, sometimes removing him from the narrative of the parable to group him with other notable sinners from the Bible, such as Mary Magdalene, Peter the apostle, King David, and the Publican (from the Parable of the Pharisee and the Publican). Rubens paints the prodigal in the familiar pose of penitence—kneeling, with his eyes cast up toward heaven and his hands clasped to his chest. Unlike Murillo, however, who placed his returning prodigal in the center of the picture, Rubens relegates his protagonist to the lower right-hand corner of the canvas, taking advantage of the farmyard setting to combine a religious subject with an expansive genre scene. While the prodigal repents, an attractive young woman feeds the pigs for him and looks admiringly at his muscled torso (shown to good advantage by his partial undress). Her husband, meanwhile, jealously observes the scene from behind a pillar. In the foreground a sow suckles her piglets (and an opportunist dog) and in the background the figure of a horse and rider recede into the distance, a prefiguration of the prodigal's own journey home. Ostensibly showing a single moment in the parable,

SIR PETER PAUL RUBENS, *THE PRODIGAL SON*
c. 1618, oil
Koninklijk Museum voor Schone Kunsten, Antwerpen (België)

The parable's protagonist is almost squeezed out of the picture by the superabundance of additional detail in Rubens's genre scene. The landscape that opens up in the distance, however, hints of the prodigal's imminent spiritual release.

Rubens thus succeeds in suggesting events earlier on in the story (the prodigal's waywardness) as well as subsequent ones (his return to his father's house).

Not every artist sought Rubens' narrative concision, and some preferred instead to recount the parable in a sequence of individual tableaux. In addition to his work at the Hospital de la Caridad, Murillo painted the Parable of the Prodigal Son in six scenes for a private patron, and the Italian artist Luca Giordano completed a similarly extended cycle of the story (see pp. 76-81). Giordano's paintings begin with the Prodigal Son receiving his inheritance, which he promptly squanders in the next scene. The prodigal's riotous living was included by both Murillo and Giordano in their cycles, but was unusual in Counter-Reformation art, as its portrayal of prostitutes and debauchery contravened the Council of Trent's prohibition of lewd subjects in art. The profligacy of the prodigal was indicated by the corruption of his five senses: smell, sight, hearing, touch, and taste. The young rake sates himself with fancy food and copious drinking; he listens to profane music, his eyes distracted by the luxurious silver tableware, and while all this is going on, he appreciatively embraces the ample bosom of his female companion. But the prodigal's pleasures are curtailed in the following picture, which shows him being hounded out of town by his boon companions, one of whom stoops down to pick up rocks to throw at the newly destitute young man. The prodigal's repentance is represented in two scenes—first among the swine and then again at his father's house—and the sequence concludes with the feast of the fatted calf. A counterpart to the "riotous living" table scene, the "fatted calf" stresses the community aspect of the feast and its probity in celebrating an appropriate occasion.

The popularity of parable subjects in seventeenth-century art found its greatest expression in the work of another Italian artist, Domenico Fetti. Born in Rome c. 1588, Fetti was appointed official court painter to Ferdinando Gonzaga, Duke of Mantua, while still in his early twenties and he held the post virtually up until his death in 1623. It was during this period that he completed his extensive sequence of parable paintings, fourteen works in all, although two of the paintings are more properly regarded as portrayals of parabolic sayings—the Mote and the Beam and the Blind Leading the Blind. Fetti's choice of the latter saying was perhaps influenced by Breughel's painting of the same subject (see pp. 96–97), which was then part of the Gonzaga collection. Small in format but freely executed, the paintings were originally hung together in the small low-ceilinged apartments of Isabella d'Este, an intimate setting which would have allowed close scrutiny of their full moral import. They were evidently popular images, for additional copies/versions were made of ten of the subjects, either by Fetti himself or by his workshop. Paintings such as *The Parable of the Lost Pence* (see p. 74) betray the influence of the Italian painter Caravaggio, the startling lighting effects transforming a rather humdrum domestic occurrence into one filled with tension and even menace. The light of the lamp in the darkened room acts as a visual metaphor for the sinner's journey from spiritual darkness to enlightenment. Fetti's interpretation of *The Parable of the Lost Sheep* (see p. 40) is, by contrast, a charming pastoral scene, which concentrates on the joy of finding the lost object. The shepherd's pose is that of the Good Shepherd, and unlike the woman who is entirely absorbed in the hunt for her lost coin, he looks directly out at the viewer, inviting him to acknowledge the successful outcome of the search and to share in his happiness.

The tranquillity of this landscape scene is quickly displaced by the stark urban setting of *The Parable of the Unmerciful Servant* (see p. 45). Fetti again chooses to portray the pivotal moment of the story: the violent demand for money by the unmerciful servant.

In this composition, crumbling antique architecture frames the action and a vine winds itself around the parapet, an organic echo of the servant's strangulating grip. The assault takes place on an isolated staircase—a sordid crime with no witnesses—and the viewer is cast in the uncomfortable role of voyeur, with no option but to share the desperation of the victim, who stares out of the picture frame as if begging for help.

Soaring classical architecture provides a regal backdrop in Fetti's *The Rich Man and Lazarus* (see p. 20), which is painted with Veronese-style verve and animation. A red velvet curtain drawn to one side reinforces the artifice and self-conscious theatricality of Fetti's composition, whose exuberance is in marked contrast to Bassano's subdued low-key treatment of the same subject. Lazarus himself has a walk-on part in the foreground

REMBRANDT VAN RYN, *THE GOOD SAMARITAN*
1633, etching and burin
© British Museum

While the injured man is helped off the horse, the Samaritan negotiates with the innkeeper. A fellow guest nonchalantly eavesdrops on the transaction.

but his ragged clothes and stooped figure jar with the opulence and robust vitality of the Rich Man and his guests, and he remains, ostracized, on the scene's periphery.

An equally festive but less forbidding milieu is depicted in *The Pearl of Great Price* (see p. 36), the most genuinely vivacious of Fetti's parable pictures. The optimism of Jesus' story is captured in the hustle and bustle of a colorful market, painted with a typically Venetian love of pageantry, of action and exotic costumes. A group of merchants have gathered around the stall, tucked away in an arcade in the marketplace, to share the excitement of their colleague's discovery. In the foreground a barrow boy pauses on his journey, his curiosity stirred by the commotion at the pearl stall, but elsewhere in the picture the worldly business of the market goes on.

The tenets of Protestantism were no less exacting than those of the Catholic Church as far as artists were concerned. Working in the Protestant Netherlands of the seventeenth century, Rembrandt chose to depict numerous biblical subjects (by far the largest proportion of his work), but it was a choice dictated by himself rather than the demands of ecclesiastical patrons, and his approach remained within Calvin's dictum "Let not God's majesty, which is far above the perception of the eyes, be debased through unseemly representation." Although he did not produce them in such numbers as Fetti, parables interested Rembrandt, and his etching of *The Good Samaritan* shows the culmination of the Samaritan's care for the wounded traveler as they arrive at the inn and the innkeeper receives his advance payment. In particular, the theme of repentance frames his work. One early painting was *The Repentant Judas,* and one of his last, *The Prodigal Son* (c. 1665). In a less penitent mood, his *Self Portrait with Saskia* (1635) shows the artist carousing with his wife and has been interpreted by some as a Prodigal Son painting in which Rembrandt casts himself as the profligate heir. For many years *The Unmerciful Servant* (see p. 124) was thought to have been by Rembrandt, but has more recently been attributed to his pupil Willem Drost. Like van Hemessen (see p. 12), the painter shows the Unmerciful Servant at the moment of his reckoning, flanked on one side by a stern-faced soldier and on the other by an anxious elderly man (perhaps the servant he wronged) and facing a now-implacable master. We witness the moment when the Unmerciful Servant's fate is sealed, but his punishment remained unspecified—unlike van Hemessen's approach to the parable, which incorporates two time frames within a single panel and shows the servant being called to account in the foreground and then being dragged off to prison in the background.

Parable subjects returned to prominence in the nineteenth century, another era characterized by a strong sense of moral purpose. Religious art permeated the century, particularly the final quarter, when the High Church movement in England was at its peak and there was a revival of Catholicism in France. This religiosity was accompanied by renewed interest in Gothic art and architecture, and in Britain many churches were subjected to medievalizing "restorations" by Victorian architects. The popularity of the medieval style led to a revival of stained glass, an art that had fallen into decline since

ATTRIB. WILLEM DROST, *THE UNMERCIFUL SERVANT*
c. 1650, oil on canvas
Reproduced by the kind permission of the Trustees of the Wallace Collection

❧

Summoned before his master to account for his actions, the Unmerciful Servant anxiously clutches his hat and bows in nervous deference. A sense of foreboding pervades the painting: The fearful body language of the accused servant and the authoritative demeanor of the King leave the severity of the punishment in little doubt.

the mid-sixteenth century and whose almost obsolete techniques had to be rediscovered by its nineteenth-century neophytes. Burlison and Grylls' window of *The Dragnet* (see p. 39) demonstrates well the contemporary interest in edifying subject matter as well as the artists' own debts to fifteenth-century Flemish and English art. Their interpretation of the parable is colorful and vivid; the billowing sails of the ship in the background intensify the sense of urgency of the task being performed in the foreground—the meticulous sorting of good fish from bad. The text "So shall it be at the end of the world" makes the window's moral message unambiguous.

Some artists, rejecting the art of the Middle Ages as a model, sought to re-create the actual settings of biblical events. In earlier centuries artists had tended to contemporize the Bible, placing their representations squarely within the context of their own times. Driven by a desire for greater realism, artists now traveled to the Holy Land to observe firsthand the original locale. The Pre-Raphaelite painter Holman Hunt made several trips there between 1854 and 1904, his last visit being the year before he painted *The Importunate Neighbour* (see p. 69). The parable provided Hunt with the opportunity of painting a night scene (the challenges of which had long fascinated him, as in *The Light of the World*), as well as the moralizing subject matter he preferred. Importuned by his unexpected guests, the protagonist of the parable has—still barefooted—run over to ask his neighbor for some bread. Leaning against the door in desperation, the man tries to rouse his neighbor, who has yet to respond to his knocking. In the meantime, beyond the starlit courtyard, lights in the windows and doorway of his own house glimmer invitingly through the palm trees—a reminder of the hungry visitor awaiting his return.

The diversity of religious art in the nineteenth century is encapsulated in the work of the French artist James Tissot. Best known as a painter of fashionable beauties and "modern life," Tissot, like Rembrandt before him, was fascinated by the story of the Prodigal Son and returned to it at different times in his life. His first attempt at the subject illustrated the departure and the return of the prodigal in a medieval setting and was ill-received. Historicism was evidently in the air and critics found the paintings "affected, false and artificial." Some years later Tissot changed tack and expanded the parable into four paintings of *The Prodigal Son in Modern Life*. These proved more popular, winning Tissot a gold medal when he showed them at the Exposition Universelle in Paris in 1889 and ensuring the success of the etchings he made on the same subject. The setting of the series is extremely contemporary—the prodigal's exile in Japan reflects the late-nineteenth-century mania for all things Japanese and transforms the harlots into exotic geishas. The return is given a downbeat London dockside location, a cargo of pigs and other livestock neatly alluding to the prodigal's recent lowly occupation. The feast scene takes place in a rather more glamorous Thameside setting, this time a rural one in which Tissot, ever topical, manages to incorporate the fashionable middle-class pastime of boating.

Tissot's work took another direction when, in 1885, he had a vision while painting in the church of St. Sulpice in Paris. The experience left him determined to dedicate himself to the (self-appointed) task of illustrating the life of Christ. Like Holman Hunt before him, Tissot set off for the Holy Land to fulfill his vision and spent some time there painting and drawing from the motif, interviewing scholars and locals, and amass-

James Tissot, *L'Enfant Prodigue: Le Départ, En Pays Etranger, Le Retour,* and *Le Veau Gras*
1881, drypoint
Gift of George A. Goddard, June 1919, courtesy Museum of Fine Arts, Boston

ing a formidable array of notes. On his return to France, Tissot worked up his material into 365 finished illustrations, and the result of his endeavor was published in France in 1896–97 as *The Life of Our Savior Jesus Christ: 365 Compositions from the Four Gospels.* An English edition was subsequently published and proved particularly influential in the early years of the twentieth century when motion pictures took on the mantle of Bible narrator. Tissot's Bible was consulted by the filmmaker D. W. Griffith, who used the illustrations as source material for the costumes and settings of his 1916 film, *Intolerance.*

Tissot's *Life of Christ* was just one of many illustrated Bibles and religious books produced during the nineteenth century. Thanks to the development of wood-block printing, it was possible to produce thousands of images without reducing the quality of the image (in the past, the metal printing plates would wear out), and at the same time, improved education and the growth of the middle class meant that a wider readership than ever before could be reached. For all the advancements, though, Bible illustrations still performed the same role as those in the very earliest Bibles: helping to explain the text as well as adorning it. Publishers produced Bibles for every pocket; some editions, such as Tissot's, were luxury products, while others, such as Cassell's *Family Bible,* were more affordable. Published in four volumes between 1859 and 1863, the *Family Bible* included wood-engraved illustrations that were provided by a number of different artists, including Gustave Doré and Castelli. Densely illustrated, the *Family Bible* included maps and notes for the reader's further edification and was a best-seller for many years, its illustrations being particularly favored as a teaching tool by missionaries.

The strength of the market for illustrated religious texts can be gauged from the speed with which Doré was commissioned to singlehandedly illustrate an edition of the Bible. Published in 1865 by Mame et Fils, Tours (who subsequently published Tissot's *Life of Christ*), Doré's Bible (as it became known) also was very successful, and in it the artist was able to indulge to the full his love of dramatic subjects like the parables. Readers and critics alike praised the "accuracy" of his illustrations and relished the "oriental splendour" of the compositions, unaware perhaps that Doré hated traveling and had never visited the Holy Land, his "realism" relying on photographs and trips to archaeological exhibitions in Paris—and his vivid imagination.

The melodramic tendencies of Tissot's and Doré's Bible illustrations found their antithesis in the homely parable illustrations of the English Pre-Raphaelite painter John Everett Millais. Millais spent six years working intermittently on the illustrations to *The Parables of Our Lord Jesus Christ,* commissioned in 1857 by the Dalziel Brothers, the renowned wood engravers. The venture proved a laborious one, and only twenty of the thirty intended engravings were completed. Justifying his slowness to the engravers, Millais wrote of his painstaking methods, "Each parable I illustrate perhaps a dozen times before I fix and the 'Hidden Treasure' I have altered on the wood at least six times." Millais did not share Holman Hunt's zeal for topological accuracy, and while

SIR JOHN EVERETT MILLAIS, *THE PRODIGAL SON*
1864, wood engraving

In a faithful interpretation of Luke's parable, the reunion scene takes place away from the house, the father having seen his son from a distance and hastened to greet him.

some of his prints do attempt to convey an Eastern flavor, others, such as *The Sower* and *The Good Samaritan*, betray the fact that Scotland, not Palestine, had provided the landscape settings. The lack of authentic detail was criticized when the book was published, and such was the enthusiasm for archaeologically accurate reconstructions that it was even suggested that Millais should have traveled to the Holy Land. Such criticism is rather redundant today, as Millais's interpretations seem no more or less accurate than those of his fellow illustrators, and what he lacks in "oriental splendour," he makes up for in the quality of his draftsmanship and the sympathy with which he evokes the domestic, intimate quality of Jesus' parables.

Millais's wood engravings outnumber even Fetti's cycle of paintings, but a compar-

SIR JOHN EVERETT MILLAIS, *THE GOOD SAMARITAN*
1864, wood engraving

The Scottish landscape that Millais used as the setting for his parable pictures is clearly in evidence in this composition.

---

ison between the two men's work—so different in style and separated by more than three hundred years—is instructive. The moral lessons and memorable, dramatic, and, above all, human scenarios presented by Jesus' stories have a powerful visual dimension, which has inspired successive generations of Christian artists. From tentative, derivative paintings on the catacomb walls to the vibrant stained glass of medieval cathedrals to the mass-produced monochrome prints of the nineteenth century, representations of the parables reveal as much about the age in which they were produced as they do about the parables themselves. Although Christian art has continually reinterpreted the parables, such images share the original stories' capacity to provoke, puzzle, and engage their audience and remain an intrinsic yet distinctive element in Christian iconography.